A WITNESS
TO GENOCIDE

ALSO BY ROY GUTMAN

Banana Diplomacy:
The Making of an American Foreign
  Policy in Nicaragua 1981–1987

A WITNESS TO GENOCIDE

The 1993 Pulitzer Prize–winning Dispatches
on the "Ethnic Cleansing" of Bosnia

ROY GUTMAN

A LISA DREW BOOK

Macmillan Publishing Company
New York

Maxwell Macmillan Canada
Toronto

Maxwell Macmillan International
New York   Oxford   Singapore   Sydney

For Betsy and Caroline

Lisa Drew Books
Macmillan Publishing Company
866 Third Avenue
New York, NY 10022

Maxwell Macmillan Canada Inc.
1200 Eglinton Avenue East
Suite 200
Don Mills, Ontario M3C 3N1

Macmillan Publishing Company is part of the Maxwell Communication Group of Companies.

Library of Congress Cataloging-in-Publication Data
Gutman, Roy.
    A witness to genocide : the 1993 Pulitzer Prize–winning dispatches on the "ethnic cleansing" of Bosnia / Roy Gutman.
        p.   cm.
    "A Lisa Drew Book."
    ISBN 0-02-546750-6. — ISBN 0-02-032995-4 (pbk.)
    1. Yugoslav War, 1991– —Bosnia and Hercegovina—Sources. 2. Yugoslav War, 1991– —Atrocities—Sources. 3. Bosnia and Hercegovina—History, Military—Sources. I. Title.
DR1313.G88   1993
949.7'42024—dc20   93-24074   CIP

Macmillan books are available at special discounts for bulk purchases for sales promotions, premiums, fund-raising, or educational use. For details, contact:

Special Sales Director
Macmillan Publishing Company
866 Third Avenue
New York, NY 10022

DESIGN BY ERICH HOBBING

10   9   8   7   6   5   4   3   2   1

Printed in the United States of America

Acknowledgments

Events like these drive reporters on, but I could not have sustained the commitment without a bedrock of support. My wife Betsy and daughter Caroline gave unstinting encouragement despite the long absences and the missed vacations. The editors of *Newsday* and *New York Newsday,* Tony Marro, Les Payne, Howard Schneider, Bob Brandt, Don Forst, Jim Toedtman, and Jim Dooley, let me follow my instincts, then put the newspaper's reputation on the line for the stories that resulted. Jeff Sommer, the foreign editor, keeps the highest standards in the business. Our deskers, Leslie Davis and Jack Klein, fielded everything I could throw at them with grace and skill. My local associates, Seska Stanojlovic in Belgrade and Nada Kronja-Stanic in Ljubljana, proved themselves professionals whose skills and engagement were indispensable at every stage of the reporting. Andree Kaiser is a one-of-a-kind photographer, and his associate Boris Geilert is an ace. Their extraordinary pictures bear witness.

The idea for this book arose from a conversation with Simon Wiesenthal, the famed Nazi hunter, who has devoted his life to documenting genocide and bringing justice to the victims. He gave me an eloquent reason: "All of us need an alibi so that we can say we were not silent, that we informed people, that we did everything to bring knowledge about this to the public." His associate, Helen Fein of the Institute for the Study of Genocide in Cambridge, Massachusetts, provided quick and ample documentation, as did Vanessa Vasic of the esteemed Balkan War Report in London. James Gow of Kings College, London, Patrick Moore of Radio Free Europe, Saul Friedman of *Newsday*'s Washington bureau, and Jim Klurfeld, the editor of the editorial pages, made timely and helpful suggestions for the introduction.

Heidi Ewich, the office manager in the *Newsday* Bonn bureau, worked endless hours organizing my travels, running the office and spurring me on. Our next-door neighbors, Chrystel and Albert Luetzen, adopted my family as their own in my absence.

I must also express gratitude to the brave and honest souls who carry on the international relief effort, and who always found time to brief me. So they can continue their work, they shall remain nameless. The stories owe themselves to the Bosnians of every national origin who facilitated every step I took—men and women who endured unspeakable suffering who mustered the self-confidence and the trust to tell a foreign reporter what had happened to them and their families. My wish for the survivors of this scourge is that justice will one day be theirs.

Author's Note

"Please try to come here. There is a lot of killing. They are shipping Muslim people through Banja Luka in cattle cars. Last night there were 25 train wagons for cattle crowded with women, old people and children. They were so frightened. You could see their hands through the openings. We were not allowed to come close. Can you imagine that? It's like Jews being sent to Auschwitz. In the name of humanity, please come."

The voice at the other end of the telephone was a Muslim political leader in Banja Luka, the second largest city in Bosnia-Herzegovina. It was July 9, 1992.

I had visited Banja Luka in November 1991 to take the political pulse in the future capital of Bosnia's secessionist Serb minority. Mayor Predrag Radic handed me a color-coded map showing a Serb-controlled land corridor to Belgrade across territory inhabited mainly by Muslims and Croats in northern Bosnia. It made clear that Bosnian Serbs with the backing of their cousins in Serbia were preparing a full-scale war of conquest.

The war that began in April 1992 was predictable. What no one could have imagined were the atrocities against Muslim and Croat civilians for which the Serbs invented the euphemism "ethnic cleansing." Because reporters could not move about freely, the only way to reconstruct events was to question refugees who were flooding out of Bosnia. Their stories of arbitrary executions and wholesale deportations were chilling, but what alarmed me most were signs that the Yugoslav army, which had transformed itself into the Bosnian Serb army, was overseeing the operation. Meanwhile, the government of Serbia, which had territorial ambitions against the newly independent Bosnia-Herzegovina, was providing logistical support. That suggested a plan and the organization to implement it on a massive scale. I had no idea how to uncover and document the bigger picture but assumed there would be many leads.

No one could have been more surprised than I to be investigating the possibility of genocide in the former Yugoslavia. As a wire service correspondent in Belgrade in the early 1970s, I had learned the language, gotten to know the country and its politics, and made many friends. I had felt at home in Serbia and in Yugoslavia in general. That land had changed beyond recognition. It was while transiting Zagreb, the Croatian capital, with a U.S. relief flight to Sarajevo in early July that I got a tip that Serbs had begun full-scale "cleansing" in Banja Luka. That would have been a frightening prospect, affecting upwards of 90,000 people, and it prompted my phone calls.

Early in July the Serb-led army opened the war corridor depicted on Mayor Radic's map, and we were on the second bus convoy to Banja Luka. "We" were a tight but unique team: Seska Stanojlovic, an exceptional Yugoslav journalist-interpreter with overseas reporting experience, and Andree Kaiser, a gifted freelance photographer from Germany. The 14-hour journey took us through combat zones, past destroyed villages and towns, over makeshift army bridges. On arriving in Banja Luka the organizers dumped us in a sports hall and told us to sleep on the floor because it was after curfew.

The city of 200,000 was unscathed by any fighting, but it was full of grizzled fighters of every age and in a dozen different uniforms, carrying submachine guns, rifles, pistols and knives. But on the civil side there was still a semblance of order. "Ethnic cleansing" had not really begun here. I called on the mayor and the military spokesman, who both said they had no information on deportations. Muslim and Croat officials, by comparison, had kept careful records, with times, dates and details. By virtue of being the first Western reporter on the scene and asking the question, I obtained confirmations of the deportations in boxcars from the Bosnian Serb Red Cross and the chief of police. Police Chief Stojan Zupljanin had a casual explanation for the reversion to Third Reich practices: "None of the refugees asked for first-class carriages."

That three-day visit provided the tips that led to two other major stories, on mass murder in Serb-run concentration camps and systematic rape by the conquering forces. Muslim and Croat politicians had been collecting reports about detention camps set up by the Serbs around northern Bosnia, the most notorious of them at Omarska, an open-pit iron mine north of Banja Luka. "I will tell you about the living conditions in the camps," said a Muslim official. "All the grass has been eaten by the people. Every day in Omarska between 12 and 16 people die. In the first six days they don't receive any food. There is no possibility of any visit. No possibility of packages. No medical help. Two-thirds of them are living under the open skies. It is like an open pit. When it rains, many of them are up to their knees in mud." I went straight to the army headquarters, where I discovered something unexpected.

The best guide to what the Serbs were doing came from their own propaganda.

At the headquarters in Banja Luka, Major Milovan Milutinovic sat behind a portable typewriter churning out lurid diatribes. "Under such a hot, Balkanic sky," began one tract, "necklaces have been strung of human eyes and ears, skulls have been halved, brains have been split, bowels have been torn out, human spits and children's bodies have been pierced by bayonets, once again have become a part of the Serbian people's enemies' folklore." The document was titled "Lying [sic] Violent hands on the Serbian Woman," and its main allegation was that Muslims and Croats were committing genocide against the Serbs. It claimed this was "the third genocide against the Serbs in this century," the others being 1914 and 1941.

The tract accused Muslim authorities of launching a jihad or holy war against Serbs, of setting up detention camps in cities they controlled and leaving Serbs there "without food, water and elementary victuals." Taken literally, it made no sense. I viewed the propaganda as a coded message for the army and the paramilitary bands operating under loose army supervision. The key sentence was missing: "This is war, and if they're doing this to us, we'll do it to them." In the Balkans, where revenge is part of the code of honor, it went without saying. It was a green light for atrocities.

The text continued: "By order of the Islamic fundamentalists from Sarajevo, healthy Serbian women from 17 to 40 years of age are being separated out and subjected to special treatment. According to their sick plans going back many years, these women have to be impregnated by orthodox Islamic seeds in order to raise a generation of janissaries on the territories they surely consider to be theirs, the Islamic republic. In other words, a fourfold crime is to be committed against the Serbian woman: to remove her from her own family, to impregnate her by undesirable seeds, to make her bear a stranger and then to take even him away from her."

That was the written version. Milutinovic gave me a shorter rendition in his command briefing, the most bizarre I ever heard from a military man. What raised my eyebrows was the reference to janissaries. These were the Turkish military elite composed of Christian youth forced to convert to Islam in the Middle Ages. I tried to suppress a grin. "Which century are you talking about?" I asked. He replied: "It is a new and recent phenomenon. This is a crime against women. It has ugly aims that can hardly be imagined in the civilized world. They are trying to do what they did centuries ago."

I made a mental note to search for evidence of Serb camps of the same description. Milutinovic refused to take me to Omarska, saying he could not guarantee my safety, a transparent excuse coming from the supreme powers in charge of the region. He offered a trip to another location, the army-run prisoner-of-war camp at Manjaca. In a field just before the camp entrance, Andree and I saw a haunting scene: emaciated men with their heads shaved in a field building a perimeter fence. We looked at each other and didn't say a word. Andree was born in East Germany and had been jailed for three years for carrying a banner at a political protest. In jail he had learned the art of *runter-schrauben,* which means roughly to burrow into the background, and this he did throughout the visit. From the camp forecourt we could see at the top of a rise several hundred yards away dozens of prisoners lined up to have their heads shorn like sheep. Half a dozen guards surrounded Andree to ensure he took only authorized photos. While I talked with camp doctors, Andree passed out cigarettes to the guards and feigned boredom. When no one was looking, he snapped three frames of the prisoners on the hill. It is one of the most famous photos of the war in Bosnia, depicting the humiliation wrought on the Muslims by their conquerors. I sensed that he had a special motive in getting that photo, that of the former prisoner getting even.

While we were at Manjaca, Seska was phoning the police chief and checking out other tips. A Serb by birth, she had worked much of her career for the Croatian daily *Vjesnik,* including several years in Beijing, until she was fired as part of the newspaper's own "ethnic purification" program. When I asked how we could possibly be uncovering these things, she recalled the Serbian saying: *"Sila Bogu ne moli."* Power does not pray to God.

That afternoon I met a group of teenage boys who had just been released from Manjaca. Nothing the army told me in the morning was borne out. These were not prisoners of war but underage civilians caught in a vast roundup. Beatings and torture were routine. Few died at Manjaca, it was true. The army released the prisoners who were about to die. I met the teenagers at a funeral for one such prisoner.

By this time I sensed that the story was of such dimensions and seriousness that every element had to be sourced, using eyewitnesses or official statements, and that photos were essential to establish instant credibility. Every theory I developed about the events and those responsible should be potentially falsifiable—that is, structured in a way that if it was wrong, it could be so proven.

Having set such lofty standards, I immediately made an exception and wrote about the Omarska camp, which I had not visited, based on the secondhand witness account. The witness was too scared to talk with me directly, but her account had so startled the Muslim leadership in Banja Luka that I asked them to dictate their notes to me. My thought was that if Omarska was a death camp, this needed to be put in print to alert others. There might be no way to report it from the scene, but a printed account by an experienced reporter in a serious newspaper should arouse interest in official Washington. At my request, colleagues in the *Newsday* bureau alerted every major government agency.

No one responded. How I was to report the story became a burning question. Jeff Sommer, the *Newsday* foreign editor, made the suggestion, which may seem obvious but wasn't at the time, to return to the area. Andree and I went to Zagreb, Croatia, the single biggest collecting point for refugees from northern Bosnia. Seska had returned to Belgrade, and another indefatigable journalist, Australian-born freelancer Nada Kronja-Stanic, took over as investigator, interpreter and fixer. Within a few days we found a devoted volunteer from the Bosnian Red Crescent, a sociologist named Musadik Borogovac who had assembled a team of experts to collect data on "ethnic cleansing."

"This story will make a difference," I said to him. "We know that something terrible is going on in the camps. We must find out just what it is. Find me witnesses." After a week of searching and a number of false starts, he located former detainees from camps at Omarska and Brcko Luka. Both agreed to be photographed, but one insisted on a pseudonym to protect a son still held at Omarska.

The story they told of routine daily slaughter in the camps was explosive. *Newsday* is a tabloid with a circulation of more than 800,000 in Long Island and metropolitan New York. Its reputation derives from solid local and national reporting and a pioneering investigative unit rather than from its small team of foreign correspondents, but it had just won the Pulitzer Prize for International Reporting. The editors of *Newsday* decided to give the story the dramatic cover treatment that only a tabloid can. THE DEATH CAMPS OF BOSNIA read the headline in two-inch-high letters. It was a daring decision. The report was immediately picked up by news wires, television and radio in the United States and around the world.

A few days later a television team from the British network ITN convinced the Banja Luka authorities to provide access to Omarska. The guards allowed them to photograph some prisoners being rushed through meals. At Trnopolje, another camp, they were shown emaciated prisoners behind barbed wire who appeared to be near death. The ITN team did not realize that the authorities had moved these prisoners from Omarska a day or so earlier. Omarska had been closed. I learned this two months later on meeting released prisoners in Britain, some at the Karlovac in southern Croatia.

Something about the world reaction did not sit right. Since when in the age of spy satellites does a reporter come up with such a scoop? After all, U.S. intelligence or UN organizations must have had some information and could have disclosed the practices in the camps weeks if not months earlier. I began to develop a theory that the Western governments had written off Bosnia and had not bothered to tell the public. Media reports such as mine represented so much inconvenience. The assault against Bosnia had all the earmarks of genocide, but no official would utter the word because it would force them to come up with a policy response. So there was no official confirmation, and public interest diminished. Indeed, the acting secretary of state publicly raised doubts about the entire story. Without doubting my reporting, Sommer suggested bearing in mind the value of taking another look at the camps. Surprisingly, few if any of my colleagues followed suit.

So I went back to Serb-controlled Bosnia in mid-September and learned that 360 reporters had visited since my August 2 report. The regime had relaxed for reporters. I visited Omarska for the first time, saw Manjaca again, located camp survivors in several countries abroad and redid the story from scratch. Omarska was a death factory. Not everybody who went there died, but if it had not been closed down, the thousands there at the end of July would have been dead in a few weeks. U.S. government interviewers concluded that Serb guards killed as many as 5,000 men at Omarska of the 13,000 or so who were processed there.

While searching for camp survivors in Zagreb in late July, I called on the head of the Muslim community in Croatia, a distinguished cleric named Sevko Omerbasic. He was at his wit's end. There were so many refugees, so many problems, such a huge tragedy for his people, so little interest in the West. I asked him what was known about the systematic rape of Muslim women in camps. He told me the story that at the end of June a group of mothers had arrived in Tuzla in central Bosnia on foot, after crossing minefields at the front lines, devastated because their children had been taken away from them. "Where are our daughters?" they cried. The tragedy began June 11 when Serb forces took the men to a concentration camp at Brcko on the Sava River. Then they took away the mothers. Finally they raped the daughters and released them to cross through minefields to see their mothers in Tuzla.

My editors agreed the trip was worth taking even though it meant up to two weeks without any telephone contact, and there was no certainty I could get the story. Andree and I drove to Tuzla in a four-wheel-drive vehicle from Split, a four-day journey across roads newly hacked out of mountain paths, guided by a police officer and clerk from Zvornik, a town the Serbs had overrun.

The young rape victims were packed with other refugees in every available public building. They had given interviews to Tuzla radio and willingly met me to answer questions, but photographs seemed out of the question. I enlisted the help of Jusuf Sehic, head of the Muslim charity Merhamet, and his very capable English-speaking assistant Nejira Nalic. With one exception, a young woman I had interviewed in Split a few days earlier, I had never talked with a rape victim. I bore in mind that the crime was not just moral but political, and someone had to tell her story if the world was to act to stop it. It was the same argument I used with them. We met about 20 mothers and 20 daughters together and asked them to narrate what occurred. Andree was into *runterschrauben* and remained there until the next day when the young women assembled for the photographs in the gymnasium in which so many were sleeping. First the mothers and the daughters, then as they split up, the daughters alone. Almost everyone in the room burst into tears, Andree as well. I kept on thinking that it could have been my daughter there.

Newsday gave the story dramatic cover play, but few other publications followed suit. Not until a German television program, "Mona Lisa," broadcast its own interviews in mid-November did the European public take notice. Andree's photos became covers for *Stern* magazine, *Newsweek,* and many other publications. Suddenly there was a new round of public outrage, and international relief agencies, women's groups, and parliaments sent missions to Zagreb. Few spent time in the interior; few devoted the planning, resources and time to learning the truth. And governments once again found ways to manage and dampen the outcry.

The outcome of all the reporting and the evidence gathered is mixed. Some believe that the news media have "hyped" the story, that is, overdramatized it. The judgment is based on ignorance. The facts are there, painstakingly unearthed.

The accounts speak for themselves.

Introduction

The seven politicians who led the industrial world had a lot to commiserate about in early July 1992 as they toasted each other in Munich's baroque splendor. Their economies were a mess; their careers were on the line; and the last thing they wanted was to get dragged into the dirty war just 400 miles to the south. They ended their annual summit with the promise to consider the use of military force to ensure the delivery of food aid to Bosnia-Herzegovina; but as he was leaving town, President George Bush let down his guard to reveal what he really thought of the war. It was a mere hiccup. "I don't think anybody suggests that if there is a hiccup here or there or a conflict here or there that the United States is going to send troops," he said. Not far from the palatial quarters where the Western leaders met, their predecessors 54 years earlier had signed a treaty approving Nazi Germany's carving up of Czechoslovakia, then the last functioning democracy in Eastern Europe. This time, there was no document, but the impact was the same.

Some hiccup.

In Sarajevo, several hundred thousand residents huddled in basement shelters to escape the Serb artillery. In northern Bosnia, Serb artillery and aircraft were attacking Muslim and Croat towns in their drive to open a military corridor from Belgrade to Banja Luka. Everywhere else, Serb "ethnic cleansing," the euphemism for murder, rape, and torture, was continuing against Muslims and Roman Catholic Croats. The Serb onslaught had displaced two million civilians and left tens of thousands dead. It was the most vicious conflict seen in Europe or nearly anywhere else since World War II. But the steam had run out of Bush's presidency, and he was distracted by a lackluster campaign and the economic downturn. Military advisers told him a definitive response to the bloodshed in Bosnia, which would be completed before election day, was not available. So Bush struck a pose of indifference and remained aloof even when reality intruded. In August 1992, after *Newsday* published eyewitness accounts of systematized murder in Serb concentration camps, Bush expressed shock but went on to describe the war—incorrectly—as a blood feud arising from ancient animosities. To justify his inaction, Bush revised history. Balkan politicians do it all the time. At home his statements added confusion to the public debate, but in Belgrade, the Serbian capital, the sophisticated political operators managing the war got the message. George Bush was using their rhetoric.

Ancient animosities were not the cause of the conflict. This was the third in a series of wars launched by Serbia, the powerful militarized state that emerged from the ruins of multinational Yugoslavia. Serb propaganda variously portrayed it as a civil war, even though only one side had arms and was fighting, or as an ethnic struggle or even a religious war. But the bottom line was that Serbia had harnessed the powerful military machine of the Yugoslav state to achieve the dream of its extreme nationalists: a Greater Serbia. The evidence pointed to attempted genocide against Bosnia's Muslims and Croats.

The events that led to the war were not so simple, but there was no reason to make them up.

The history of the peoples of the Balkans is a tangle of legend and myth, of claims and counterclaims over who did what to whom and when. But in Bosnia-Herzegovina, a republic of 4.4 million, there was no inherent hostility between Eastern Orthodox Serbs, mostly farmers and shepherds living in the hills who amounted to 31 percent of the population, and the Muslim Slavs, who included a secular, educated elite and constituted 44 percent. Extreme Serb nationalists in neighboring Serbia used the mystique surrounding Serbia's defeat in Kosovo Polje to the medieval Turkish empire and asserted that the Serbian nation would henceforth protect itself; but Kosovo Polje was six centuries ago, in 1389. No serious interethnic quarrels had disturbed the peace for nearly half a century in Bosnia-Herzegovina, and only the most primitive mind could justify an assault on Slavic Muslims as revenge for the fourteenth-century defeat and the subsequent five centuries of Turkish rule. On the contrary, Sarajevo, with its skyline of minarets, church steeples and synagogues, was testimony to centuries of civilized multiethnic coexistence. It was a place of learning and of commerce, a westward-looking city in an exotic setting created over the centuries: a European jewel. This was the site of the Olympics in 1984, with an ancient bazaar where young people in blue jeans drank Turkish coffee to the strains of pop music in the cobblestoned marketplace. An atmosphere of secular tolerance characterized the entire republic. Bosnia-Herzegovina was a genuine melting pot. That civilization was under attack.

America's "hands-off" approach to Yugoslavia in dissolution stood in contrast to the West's attitude for much of this century. World War I began in Sarajevo, triggered by shots fired by a Bosnian Serb determined to oust the newly installed Austrian colonial power. The assassination of Archduke Franz Ferdinand ignited an explosion that was well primed. Two Balkan wars had just been fought over dividing the spoils of the Turkish empire, and a network of alliances came into play in the tense aftermath, pitting Imperial Germany and Imperial Austria-Hungary on the one side and France, Britain, Serbia and Russia on the other to take the spoils. Preferring isolation, the United States got dragged in nevertheless. As the war drew to a close, U.S. President Woodrow Wilson crusaded for a united southern Slav state, which came into being with British and French support and was named the kingdom of the Serbs, Croats and Slovenes. The United States retreated into isolation, and the kingdom, renamed Yugoslavia in 1929, collapsed because of tensions between Serbs and Croats. The Germans took full advantage. When Serbia's crown prince Paul, the regent of Yugoslavia, seemed ready to come to terms with Nazi Germany, Serb military officers, partly at British instigation, overthrew him in a coup. The Wehrmacht made fast work of Serbia, conquering the republic in about a week. Hitler installed a puppet regime in Belgrade and made a triumphal visit to Zagreb, the capital of Croatia, where he sponsored the fascist Ustasha regime.

At the start of World War II the Allies focused their hopes on Serb Royalist forces, known as the Chetniks. By 1943, Winston Churchill, the British prime minister, concluded that the Chetniks were collaborating with Axis powers. He then threw his support behind the partisan force headed by Josip Broz Tito, a communist of Croat-Slovene origin, which was actively resisting the Germans.

"Tito" was his nom de guerre, derived, it is thought, from *"ti to,"* the Serbo-Croatian words for "you do this." With courage, charisma and cunning, Tito united Serbs, Croats, Slovenes, Muslims and others to defeat the German occupiers and create a postwar Yugoslavia under communist rule where each nationality would live in full national rights.

Having liberated itself from the Germans with minimal help from Stalin's Soviet Union, Tito's Yugoslavia in time evolved into the world's freest communist regime. It had six republics: Bosnia-Herzegovina, Croatia, Macedonia, Montenegro, Serbia and Slovenia, as well as two autonomous provinces in Serbia, Kosovo in the south, inhabited mainly by ethnic Albanians, and Vojvodina in the north, inhabited by a mixture of every nation in Yugoslavia. Innovative economic reforms, the opening of trade, tourism and economic contacts with Western Europe, and the introduction of some civil freedoms raised the standard of living to near-West European levels. Tito kept the lid on ethnic squabbles through the mechanism of an omnipresent

Communist Party and a police apparatus. The West was not always enamored of the nonaligned movement Tito helped launch nor of his methods of suppressing dissent, but its strategic priority was to keep the Soviet Union out of the region. Over the decades the West discouraged anti-Tito forces abroad or at home who might have organized a democratic alternative to Tito's strongman regime. In the 1970s the West staked billions of dollars in guaranteed credits on an independent Yugoslavia.

In hindsight, Tito's greatest failing was that he suppressed national passions and papered over the past. No objective history has been written of the Yugoslav civil war, which coincided with World War II. Serbs assert they fought with the Allies, and this was true for many Serbs at various times and places. But the Serb claim that Croats and to a lesser extent Muslims were on the side of the Axis is self-serving, for in the shifting alliances, members of all groups had fought on all sides. Today there are no agreed-upon facts except that at least one million Yugoslavs died in the war, most within the Serb and Croat communities. Many independent experts estimate that the fascist Ustasha regime executed 70,000 to 100,000 Serbs, Jews and Gypsies at Jasenovac, a notorious concentration camp in southern Croatia. Serb nationalists speak of one million, but Croat leader Franjo Tudjman wrote it was as few as 30,000. Without an agreed figure, there was no way to channel the debate, and Jasenovac became a rallying cry for Serb nationalists. Muslims say they lost 85,000 to 100,000, making them, per capita, the principal victims of the war. Many died in an attempted genocide by Serbian Chetniks that was never acknowledged as such in the Tito era.

The constitution Tito drew up in 1974 was a Rube Goldberg construction that assumed communists would retain power forever and that the party, backed by the army, could settle all differences. It addressed national rivalries through mechanical means, by creating a collective presidency for the post-Tito era and rotating top positions among six republics and two Serbian provinces. Yet the system prevented the emergence of institutions or a truly national leader who could carry on Tito's balancing act. Tito himself had banished from political life some of the ablest of his potential successors. After ousting a generation of Croatian communists who came to power on a wave of Croatian national feeling in 1971, Tito then turned to Serbia and for the sake of even-handedness ousted and disgraced a generation of liberal-thinking technocrats. After his death in 1980, politicians, including many who had served jail terms for their nationalist writings in the Tito era, won elections by appeals to national identity.

Slobodan Milosevic, a Serb communist, was the first politician to grasp that the Tito era was over. The son of an Orthodox priest and Serb mother who both committed suicide, he rose through the ranks of the Serb national Beobanka, working in New York and Belgrade. He became social friends with the U.S. ambassador to Belgrade in the late 1970s, Lawrence Eagleburger. After Eagleburger retired from government service, Serbian state contracts went to the consulting firm that Eagleburger had joined, Henry Kissinger Associates.

Milosevic was a brilliant tactician and rose to prominence by seizing control of the major news media and ruthlessly stirring up nationalist hatred against Albanians, who are the vast majority of the population of Kosovo. He did not invent nationalism or the expansionist demand for a greater Serbia, but opportunistically he took up a cause made respectable by Serb intellectuals in a 1986 memorandum that claimed Serbs were the losers in Tito's Yugoslavia. Milosevic's tactic was to stage massive public rallies and demonstrations against Albanians in Kosovo. On a wave of national support he seized direct control of Kosovo, instituted a brutal crackdown on its leaders, and replaced the Kosovo member on the rotating presidency. He did the same in Vojvodina. And Milosevic manipulated elections in tiny Montenegro, most of whose 600,000 population are ethnic Serbs, to ensure that he controlled the parliament. He thus single-handedly destroyed the constitutional order.

Serbs are the largest population of the Yugoslav nations, with six of the nine million in Serbia proper, about 1.4 million in Bosnia-Herzegovina, and 600,000 in Croatia. After stirring up Serbs outside Serbia to demand protection, Milosevic repeatedly won elections by claiming he alone would protect Serb rights. He also raised wages on the eve of key elections by raiding the state treasury.

Communism collapsed in Yugoslavia as elsewhere in Eastern Europe due to corruption scandals, ineptitude and the fatigue that comes from being in power a half-century. The Communist Party, fortified by the Yugoslav Peoples' Army, had been the all-nationalities glue that kept the country together. Serbs, who more than any other ethnic group fomented the breakup, were poised to seize the assets of the state, headquartered in Belgrade, and even more important, the military. During 45 years of peace the army, one of Europe's biggest, had acquired an immense stockpile of conventional weapons to defend against a mythical Soviet bloc attack. Serbs and their Montenegrin cousins had always dominated the army's officer corps, and Milosevic set about manipulating the army into become his personal instrument.

Milosevic's demagoguery and power aggrandizement stirred popular anger, especially in the wealthier western republics, Slovenia and Croatia. With ample public support their leaders called for western-style political and economic reforms, which widened the rift with authoritarian Serbia. They also proposed, with the backing of Bosnia-Herzegovina and Macedonia, a loose confederal system to replace federal Yugoslavia. Milosevic rejected all compromises.

The last straw for the constitution, for the state and for the peoples of Yugoslavia was in May 1991 when Milosevic used his stolen votes on the collective presidency to block the routine rotation of the president's position to a Croat named Stipe Mesic. Simultaneously on June 25, Croatia and Slovenia declared their independence.

Although Milosevic takes most of the blame for what followed, it is hard to see how he could have launched a series of wars without the acquiescence of the United States and Western Europe. The West had treated Yugoslavia as a unique case during the Cold War, but after the collapse of communism it became secondary to the main preoccupation, the breakup of Mikhail Gorbachev's Soviet empire. A consensus formed at the State Department and in Western Europe chancelleries not to support any steps in Yugoslavia that would encourage the breakup of the Soviet empire. Pentagon officials argued that a peaceful dissolution of the Soviet Union was desirable and that Yugoslavia's dissolution, if directed peacefully, would set the right example. The Pentagon lost the internal debate. Bush's decision was misguided on both fronts. The most charitable explanation was that events in the heady days of the collapse of communism had outpaced the ability of the U.S. government to formulate policy. As early as 1990 the U.S. Central Intelligence Agency assessed that Yugoslavia was destined to come apart.

Personalities also made a difference. In addition to Eagleburger, who returned to government service under the Bush administration as deputy secretary of state, another old Yugoslav hand, Brent Scowcroft, became national security adviser. Scowcroft had been an air attaché in Belgrade in the early 1960s; later at Columbia University he wrote his doctoral thesis on foreign aid to Yugoslavia. While out of government during the Reagan administration, both continued their relationship with Serb and Yugoslav leaders. Eagleburger joined the board of Yugo America, the U.S. branch of the Serbia-based car manufacturer, and served as president of Henry Kissinger Associates, which had contracts with Yugo America and other Yugoslav state-owned enterprises. Scowcroft was vice president. Both spoke Serbo-Croatian, reportedly to each other on occasion, and both, according to official sources, came down on the side of the State Department in the Bush administration internal debate.

On June 21, 1991, five days before Yugoslavia dissolved, Secretary of State James Baker flew to Belgrade to announce U.S. policy. Baker said the West wanted Yugoslavia to remain united and urged Slovenia and Croatia to avoid unilateral action, warning that Washington would not recognize their independence. In the charged atmosphere, Serbs took his position as coincident with their point of view. Fully aware of what might follow, the administration then withdrew from any active role in the looming crisis. "We worry, frankly, about history repeating itself," said Baker, alluding to the conflict between the Austro-Hungarian empire and Serbia that touched off World War I.

The European Community was eager to take charge. "This is the hour of Europe," exclaimed Jacques Poos, the Luxembourg foreign minister who, as rotating chairman of the council of ministers, launched the first in a series of EC peace initiatives. But the EC was an economic grouping without a mechanism for formulating or implementing a foreign policy. It could send observers and mediators. It could impose trade or arms embargoes, but it had no institution to enforce any agreements it mediated. Only NATO, with the participation of the United States, could do that. American policy called for "containing" the fighting in Croatia, but Washington opposed the use of force to back it up.

One day after Croatia and Slovenia declared independence, rump Yugoslavia went to war against the two breakaway states. Slovenia had organized its defenses in secret over two years and routed the federal army's ill-prepared conscripts. Without any reconnaissance, tank columns rolled into ambushes set by the Slovene territorial defense. The federal army sued for peace after just 10 days. The second war, against Croatia, a mostly Roman Catholic republic with a sizable minority of Christian Orthodox Serbs, began slowly but lasted a little more than six months. Declaring independence, Tudjman, a communist general-turned-nationalist, fell into the trap Milosevic had set during his month-long public humiliation of Croatia's candidate for the collective presidency. Croatia was unprepared for war; Serbia was ready and willing. Paramilitary forces organized in Serbia began the offensive by launching artillery attacks on cities in eastern Slavonia, but after it was clear that no outside power would intervene, the army itself took the offensive in August around the major Serb enclaves in Croatia. The EC failed in repeated missions to secure a ceasefire. In September, at American and British behest, the UN Security Council imposed an arms embargo on Yugoslavia and all its component parts. The Serbs, who enjoyed an enormous advantage in weapons, were supportive.

Tudjman suppressed the bad news as long as he could and never issued an accurate death toll, but as many as 25,000 were killed or missing. The federal army's descent into barbarity stunned the world. The leveling of Vukovar, once a gracious town on the Danube, and the targeting of centuries-old monuments in Dubrovnik, Croatia's most famous tourist resort, were only the most visible signs. Serb forces detained, tortured or slaughtered thousands of Croats whose only fault was their ethnic identity and their attempt to defend their villages. The war ended in January 1992 after Serb forces had seized roughly a quarter of Croatian territory

As news media focused on the suffering and destruction in one of Europe's favorite bargain vacation lands, Germany, newly reunited and responding to public pressures, demanded that Europe act more forcefully. In response, the European Community decided to recognize Croatia and Slovenia in December 1991. Yet Germany, under its own postwar constitution, was unable to back up its initiative with force. And while recognition of Croatia possibly contributed to a ceasefire there, it also enabled Serbs to transfer the rivalry with Croatia to Bosnia-Herzegovina, a predictable consequence Bonn tried to ignore. Bosnia's Serb minority insisted on remaining part of Yugoslavia, while Muslims and Croats wanted no part of a state dominated by Milosevic and Serb nationalists. Bosnia's Serbs held a referendum in November 1991 and registered 98 percent support to remain inside Yugoslavia. The Bosnian government, on the advice of a European Community study team, held an independence plebiscite in late February 1992. Serbs boycotted it, but 99 percent of those voting favored independence.

The third war began April 6 as the United States and the European Community accorded diplomatic recognition to Bosnia-Herzegovina. In theory the new state was better off diplomatically than Slovenia or Croatia, for Bosnian leader Alija Izetbegovic had followed to the letter a plan prescribed by the United States and its European partners. Washington explicitly accepted Bosnia's "pre-crisis republic borders as the legitimate international borders." Unlike Croatia and Slovenia, Bosnia could claim to be the victim of cross-border aggression and assert the right to self-defense under the UN charter. Yet the United States and Britain chose to interpret the principles of world order selectively and decided that the September arms ban applied to the newly recognized state.

Militarily, Bosnia-Herzegovina could hardly have been worse off. Bosnia's Muslims were not the fierce Mujahedin warriors of Serb propaganda; they were mostly city dwellers, artisans, teachers, doctors, small businessmen and farmers, predominantly pacifists. Women do not wear the chador, men rarely wear a fez or attend religious services; Muslims in Bosnia viewed their religion as a national identity and saw themselves as secular Europeans first, Muslims second. Izetbegovic, a Sarajevo lawyer who had twice been jailed under the Tito regime for writing a tract advocating Muslim rights, encouraged the pacifist strain with peace rallies and marches in a naive hope of stopping the juggernaut.

The republic had long been a principal site of federal army bases, munitions plants and vast underground arsenals, and the Yugoslav army built up its presence as it withdrew from Croatia and Slovenia. In May, responding to international criticism, the federal army said it was withdrawing from Bosnia. Some forces withdrew to Serbia, but most just changed their shoulder patches and transformed themselves into the Army of the Serbian Republic. In effect, Serbia turned over the army's arsenals to local proxy forces. This gave the Serb proxy army a ten-to-one margin over the government, according to the London-based International Institute for Strategic Affairs. Worsening the odds still more was the arms embargo, whose only real application was against the Bosnian government.

Bosnia-Herzegovina did not have an army, a military tradition or weapons. It had not enjoyed independence in the modern era, but then, neither did any of the Yugoslav republics except Serbia and Montenegro. Landlocked, its supply routes were controlled by Serbia and Croatia and their proxies in Bosnia. Both Serbia and Croatia hoped to carve up the republic. Tudjman and Milosevic had met several times in 1991, and while they were totally at odds over Croatia, they were able to agree on a partition of Bosnia-Herzegovina.

From the outside it may have looked like a hopeless case, but principles were at stake, as was the existence of a European nation. Bosnia-Herzegovina, moveover, had made a unique contribution to Western civilization based on the practice of multiethnic coexistence. Western Europe faced the fundamental choice of whether to arm the government forces and intervene to preserve the territorial integrity of the republic of 4.4 million, or to partition Bosnia along ethnic lines. With the United States still passive and uninvolved,

European leaders opted for the hypocritical middle ground, recognizing territorial integrity but not committing the use of force that would uphold it. To cover up the ambiguity, foreign ministers opted for bland phrases such as a "negotiated solution." It translated into appeasement.

Just as Germany had pursued diplomacy without coercion to back it up, the European Community followed suit. The strongest measure they could agree on was economic sanctions. Willy-nilly, their ambivalence encouraged the conquerors. Portugal, the E.C.'s rotating chairman, coaxed by Peter Carrington, the former British foreign secretary, established the pattern just after Croatia and Serbia reached peace in January 1992. At a meeting in Lisbon, Serbs demanded that Bosnia-Herzegovina be split into six cantons. The European Community endorsed the plan; the Bosnian Croats gave a guarded response. Bosnia's political establishment rejected the plan, but Bosnian Croats and Serbs subsequently reaffirmed it.

By this time the Serbs could assume there would be no major obstacles to conquest provided they got it over with fast. The war in Croatia functioned as a dress rehearsal. The federal army began bombarding Sarajevo and launched a blitzkrieg campaign to seize a strip of land along the Drina River, which forms the border between Bosnia and Serbia. Then it went on to conquer a strip across northern Bosnia linking Belgrade, the capital of Serbia proper, with Banja Luka, the main city in the predominantly Serb region of northern Bosnia. The army took about 70 percent of Bosnian territory and closed all major arteries to Muslim areas.

In Drina valley towns such as Bijelina and Foca, Serb paramilitary forces crossed in from Serbia and began "ethnic cleansing." The term derived from Serb propaganda in Kosovo where nationalists claimed, without any basis, that Albanians deliberately tried to commit genocide against the region's Serbs. In Bosnia, "ethnic cleansing" became a euphemism for genocide.

The spokesman for the Serbs was Radovan Karadzic, a psychiatrist and writer who had studied poetry in a postgraduate program at Columbia University. Karadzic specialized in standing the facts on their head. He invented the rationale for the war, that Muslims would set up an Islamic republic in Bosnia, putting all Serbs at risk, a claim for which he had no evidence. Throughout the conflict Karadzic devoted his vivid imagination to inventing instant lies. If an artillery shell landed in Sarajevo killing civilians, Karadzic would claim Muslims had fired on their own people. He flatly denied that Serbs had detained any civilians or had systematically raped Bosnian women but accused the other side of doing the same. Few in the press accepted anything he said at face value, but many Western governments in search of alibis for inaction borrowed from his analysis of moral equivalency between the aggressor and the victim. Urging the Bosnian government to negotiate with Karadzic, they conveniently ignored his public demands for the expulsion of Muslims and Croats from areas Serbs claimed as their own.

Despite some compelling press reports about "ethnic cleansing," Western governments generally kept their silence. But there was no way they could ignore public reaction after television stations showed the reported Serb artillery attacks on city dwellers in a bakery queue or at the Sarajevo cemetery. On May 24, 1992, Baker called for a relief effort but no real assistance. Condemning "what truly is a humanitarian nightmare in the heart of Europe," he said the West should not consider force until it had exhausted all other remedies, and he implied that the West would treat Bosnia as an international "basket case." Yet there was no way that relief agencies like the UN High Commission for Refugees and the International Red Cross could fill the vacuum left by the West's abandonment of the new state.

The Bush administration sometimes seemed to spend more effort trying to manage the news than on the crisis itself. One such occasion was *Newsday*'s dramatic August 2 account by survivors of two death camps in northern Bosnia. At first the State Department said it had evidence of maltreatment in such camps but had no plans to do anything about it. That provoked a public furor. The next day the Department backtracked and said it had no information to support the account. Officials apparently feared that the public outcry might force changes in U.S. policy. Bush waited until after the first television pictures of emaciated prisoners shocked the world, and then he engaged in a series of calculated evasions. Calling the war against Bosnia "a blood feud" and "a complex, convoluted conflict that grows out of age-old animosities," he did not demand that the camps be closed down and the civilians be freed. He asked only for International Red Cross access to the camps.

Using their best public relations techniques, top aides expressed the notion that the war in Bosnia was a civil war in which all sides were to blame and that all sides were crazy. The State Department discouraged congressional or private delegations from going to the scene and sent none of its own. In mid-August, Eagleburger, on his way to replacing Baker as secretary of state, said a CIA investigation had found no evidence of systematic killing in the camps, only of "unpleasant conditions." He had overlooked the testimony of Alija Lujinovic before the Senate Armed Services Committee, cited in the *Newsday* account, that he had witnessed more than 1,000 executions.

The *Newsday* series in this book catalogues only some of the forms of the savagery: random slaughter, organized deportations, death camps, systematic rape and castration, and assaults on refugees fleeing for their lives. The total killed is not known but could amount to 200,000 to 250,000 through June 1993, well over 10 percent of the Muslim population. In aim and method "ethnic cleansing" amounts to genocide, as defined in the International Genocide Convention. This bans killing or harming members of a national, ethnic, racial or religious group with intent to destroy it in whole or in part or imposing measures that would prevent reproduction of the group. "Genocide has many forms," Simon Wiesenthal told this author. "You don't have to kill everyone to have genocide. This is genocide, absolutely."

Yet in dampening the outcry, the administration may have wasted an opportunity. In a small country like Serbia that ultimately wants recognition, publicity can make a difference. Within a day or so of *Newsday*'s report on death camps, the Bosnian Serbs closed Omarska, one of the biggest camps, dispersed the prisoners, and opened the facility to news media and the International Red Cross. By investigating the conditions and publicizing the truth when Serb authorities were thrown off balance, the United States and the West might have shaken the power structure of the conquerors of Bosnia. It has since become clear that top Karadzic aides had set up and run death camps and rape camps alike. But Bush and Eagleburger instead did the absolute minimum, and 10 months later the Serbs were continuing to operate detention camps and deny access to the Red Cross.

The administration was heading full speed in a different direction. By then Britain had taken the chair of the European Community and Prime Minister John Major, seeing a leadership vacuum, tried to take charge of Western policy-making.

Major called an international conference on the former Yugoslavia in London to implement a policy that had never been announced, no less debated in public. The tone was set by Eagleburger, whose keynote address spoke about the suffering of Serbs throughout history and the historic special relations between the United States and Serbia. Saying that the conflict had "ancient and complicated roots," he made no mention of the internationally recognized republic of Bosnia-Herzegovina, nor did he express hope that it would survive. It was a subtle way of saying that the Western big powers had written off the state as constituted. The conference named Cyrus Vance, the former U.S. secretary of state in the Carter administration who was representing the United Nations, and David Owen, former British foreign secretary who was representing the European Community, to organize a process for a "negotiated settlement."

Vance, a New York lawyer respected for his integrity, experience, and mediating skills, had known Owen, a quick-witted and abrasive physician-politician, from their collaboration in seeking a settlement to the Rhodesia civil war in the late 1970s. Vance was familiar with the lay of the land in Bosnia, having negotiated the truce in Croatia and the deployment of UN peacekeepers. But Vance, longtime friends noted, had a deep-seated antipathy to the use of force to solve problems. Owen had publicly advocated military strikes against Serbia. They balanced each other as they set out, but their mission was as doomed as the European Community mediation that preceded it.

They started by organizing talks with what they called the "warring parties." The Bosnian government had legitimacy but almost no arms; the Serb insurgents had arms but no legitimacy; and the much smaller Bosnian Croats' leadership had no legitimacy but the ability to block arms deliveries to the legitimate government. Vance and Owen put all three on an equal footing. In New York, Brussels and Washington, Vance and Owen campaigned to uphold the arms embargo against the Sarajevo government. According to Bosnian vice president Ejup Ganic, they promised, however, to drop their objections if Serbia rejected the proposed settlement. To attract the Bosnian Croats, Vance and Owen awarded them nearly a quarter of Bosnian territory for Croat-dominated provinces, well over their 18 percent of the population, and the territory included such cities as Mostar, Jajce, and Travnik where Muslims were the single biggest national group. Not surprisingly, Mate Boban, a Bosnian Croat nationalist who usually was chaperoned to negotiations by his patron, Franjo Tudjman, was the first to sign the accords in January 1993.

Vance and Owen had no means of coercion to back up their diplomacy, nor did they insist on ceasefires as a precondition for talks. By default they allowed the Serb military to wear down the resistance of the Bosnian government. Izetbegovic signed the accord in March 1993. The complex plan, which broke the single republic into 10 autonomous provinces—three for each of the ethnic groups and one for Sarajevo—would have ingeniously prevented the creation of a "Greater Serbia" by interposing a predominantly Croat province and a Muslim access route across the Serb corridor between Belgrade and Banja Luka. It also would have forced the Serbs to return their conquest of eastern Bosnia. Those conditions, negating the biggest war gains, made it unacceptable to the Bosnian Serbs. At the same time they failed to take into account the criticisms of the plan by newly elected American president Bill Clinton and seemed to be rushing to a fait accompli. The mediators and the new U.S. administration were undercutting each other. Vance and Owen overestimated their influence and underestimated the aggressor. Karadzic signed the document on May 2, but it was another example of the grand deception; the rest of his political colleagues rejected the plan in a series of votes in May. The mediators had no options in reserve and abandoned the plan.

The Serbs had read the signals from the UN Security Council and the Washington political scene with acuity. Economic sanctions imposed by the council against rump Yugoslavia on May 30, 1992, were one example. NATO members sent a flotilla of small warships into the Adriatic but gave them no power to stop violators, and its navies only compiled a log as ships docked at the Yugoslav port of Bar. Enforcement of the air blockade had hardly begun when the United States sought a waiver for Milan Panic, a

Serbian-born American businessman whom Milosevic brought in as prime minister of the rump Yugoslavia. Panic, who had no political experience, told the West that he would topple Milosevic, but he needed time to moderate his policies. He had a high-powered employee, John Scanlon, make the request. Scanlon was another former U.S. ambassador to Belgrade and, like Eagleburger, a member of the State Department's "Belgrade Mafia." The Bush administration endorsed his request to waive the sanctions on air travel to allow him to fly freely from country to country delivering his message, which was exactly what Western countries wanted to hear. It also raised no objections when Scanlon took on the job as Panic's national security adviser during his brief tenure in Belgrade. The United States Embassy chargé d'affaires sometimes found himself presenting notes from his government to the former U.S. ambassador. By December, Milosevic had no more use for Panic and easily ousted him in tampered elections.

By this time the enforcement of sanctions had collapsed. On land, Milosevic cronies had found so many ways around the sanctions that he managed to flood Serbia with cheap fuel and imported goods on the eve of his successful reelection campaign. Not until April, 27, 1993, 11 months later, did the Security Council approve an enforcement mechanism. Serbia found ways of violating it openly months later.

Having defined Bosnia-Herzegovina as a humanitarian problem, the West failed even to ensure food deliveries. At the Munich summit in July, Baker publicly promised to deploy U.S. air power to protect aid convoys traveling into Bosnia, but Bush listened to the objections of Colin Powell, the chairman of the Joint Chiefs of Staff, and backed away from the pledge. On August 13, 1992, the UN Security Council approved the use of military force to ensure relief deliveries in Bosnia. NATO members actually arrived to carry out the measure in late October, but under rules of engagement, in the case of Britain, that allowed them to shoot only if they could be certain of hitting their assailant. Defense Minister Malcolm Rifkind sent off Britain's 2,400 troops after warning that the government would withdraw them if they took too many casualties.

And although the Security Council banned all military flights over Bosnia on October 9, 1992, it did not impose an enforcement mechanism until six months and 465 flights later, on April 7, 1992. By the end of 1992 the State Department, from its own interviews, no longer doubted that Serbs and to a much lesser extent Croats and Muslims had carried out massive atrocities, and Eagleburger publicly released a list of names of seven top politicians or camp commanders who were potential war criminals, among them Milosevic and Karadzic. In every other respect the administration stuck with its policy.

After losing the general election to Arkansas Governor Bill Clinton in November, Bush ordered 30,000 troops to Somalia, where the United States arguably had no long-term or vital interests. Pentagon aides explained that the Joint Chiefs of Staff had themselves proposed the deployment, believing it was safer for U.S. forces to fight in the desert of Somalia than in forested mountains of Bosnia. Eagleburger stressed that because U.S. resources were limited, the deployment had no relevance for Bosnia-Herzegovina. Milosevic and Karadzic received the message they were waiting for. As U.S. troops waded ashore in Mogadishu, the Serbs stepped up the bombardment of Sarajevo and halted all aid deliveries.

Clinton was a late arrival on the scene and had few good options available when he took office in January 1993. He was badly handicapped by his own inexperience and a failure to read the diplomatic tea leaves, but that was compounded by a series of gaffes that cost him domestic political strength. Clinton's encounters with Bosnia proved as politically damaging to him as to Bosnia itself.

In his campaign Clinton had demanded tougher measures

in response to *Newsday*'s disclosure about concentration camps. "We may have to use military force," he said. "I would begin with air power against the Serbs." At his inauguration Clinton said he would use military force if there was a threat to U.S. vital interests or if "the will and conscience of the international community is defied." He made no secret of his reservations about dividing Bosnia-Herzegovina into ethnically based provinces, as proposed in the Vance-Owen plan.

Vance and Owen, Britain and France, organized a campaign to thwart Clinton's intent to use force to coerce the Serbs into a conciliation; General Powell and a little-noted but growing pro-Serbian lobby funded by U.S. Serb groups supplemented the effort in Washington that the Bosnian government failed to offset.

Confronted with a massive campaign and worried about his domestic programs, Clinton switched course by coming out in support of the Vance-Owen plan. Aides said he hoped to use the plan as a wedge to reestablish Western authority in Bosnia-Herzegovina and to that end offered to support its enforcement with troops. But again he wavered by adding the condition that all parties had to accept the negotiated settlement, thereby handing a veto on the U.S. deployment to the Bosnian Serbs. Nevertheless, Clinton encouraged Izetbegovic to sign the plan, promising to guarantee Bosnia's existence as a nation and to seek a lifting of the arms embargo if Serbia refused to sign, U.S. officials said.

The new secretary of state, Warren Christopher, who had served as Vance's deputy secretary of state in the Carter administration, unveiled a series of steps in February in a statement that suggested the Vance-Owen plan was the absolute minimum for which the United States would settle. Christopher, a San Francisco attorney whose colorless personality earned him the sobriquet "Vance's Vance," was uncharacteristically outspoken as he warned of the danger that Bosnia would lead to a wider European war:

"Beyond [the] humanitarian concerns, we have direct strategic concerns as well. The continuing destruction of a new United Nations member challenges the principle that internationally recognized borders should not be altered by force. In addition, this conflict itself has no natural borders. It threatens to spill over into new regions, such as Kosovo and Macedonia. It could then become a greater Balkan war like those that preceded World War I. Broader hostilities could touch additional nations such as Greece and Turkey and Albania . . ."

Clinton's initial experience showed that firmness worked. Against the advice of its allies and ignoring threats by Karadzic, Clinton ordered U.S. aircraft to begin air drops over eastern Bosnian enclaves where Serb forces were blocking UN relief deliveries. The civilian population received food and medicine, and at least two enclaves were temporarily saved.

Clinton continued to threaten air bombardments, and that, coupled with Christopher's tour of Europe to discuss a more vigorous approach, may have enabled Owen and Vance to bludgeon Karadzic into signing their plan on May 2. Owen proclaimed it a "great day for the Balkans." But Owen had caught the Balkan political fever of triumphalism, celebrating victory before it was complete, and publicly admonished the United States to hold off any military action until after the self-styled Bosnian Serb parliament endorsed the plan. It was a colossal miscalculation. The parliament voted down the plan and in a delaying maneuver called a referendum. Clinton, his popularity slipping at home, withdrew in exasperation from an active role.

Christopher completed the "climb-down" later that month. Declaring all sides guilty of atrocities, he trimmed his own moral argument for coming to the aid of the Bosnians. "It's been easy to analogize this to the Holocaust, but I never heard of any genocide by the Jews against the German people," he told Congress. Christopher did not explain what he had in mind, but the effect was to blame the victims for the aggression. Yet Christopher himself was partly responsible for the policy failure, for he did not try to sell the European states on air strikes but, according to congressional sources, told European leaders he, too, had reservations about shifting course.

The Vance-Owen plan was dead, American policy was in limbo, and so Owen and Norwegian diplomat Thorvald Stoltenberg, who replaced Vance in May, flew to Moscow. There Russia proposed an alternative to Vance-Owen: The United Nations should send peacekeeping forces to guard the half-dozen pockets of territory the Muslims now inhabited from the Serbian siege. Clinton gave a weak endorsement and made no commitment to provide troops for what obviously could turn into a quagmire. The Bosnian government objected to what it saw as a sellout. Karadzic welcomed the proposal.

With the West in complete disarray, the Serbs began shelling Sarajevo and the remaining Muslim enclaves in eastern Bosnia. Bosnian Croat forces with Tudjman's encouragement went on the offensive and resumed "ethnic cleansing" of Muslim towns in central Bosnia that under the Vance-Owen plan were to be Croat-dominated. In early June, Milosevic and Tudjman issued a joint call to partition Bosnia between them, leaving the Muslims in a few pockets centering on Sarajevo. Clinton said it was not his preference but raised no objections. Owen supported the plan. Vance denounced it as "the equivalent of endorsing ethnic cleansing."

The most surprising fact about Bosnia-Herzegovina was that 14 months after sustaining a blitzkrieg assault and long after Western experts had written it off, the republic was still alive. "By the classical definitions, we are supposed to be dead," Vice President Ejup Ganic quipped at the end of the first year of fighting. He said he had no idea how long the population could hold out. People fighting for their lives, their families and their land are highly motivated, however poorly armed. Humanitarian aid had kept many alive. At the same time there were many signs that the Serbs had sat on their military advantage and mounted few infantry assaults, and their chief tactic was that of the overequipped bully, shooting at villages and cities with long-range artillery. Many Western military experts ignored the political realities on the ground and focused on the "bean count," the numerical advantage the Bosnian Serbs enjoyed in the field. "I think there has been too much overestimating," of the Serb military capability, said General John Shalikashvili, the NATO supreme commander, in mid-June. Conquering Yugoslavia, he noted, "wasn't a very lengthy campaign for the Germans. The Germans did it very quickly, very efficiently."

While the Serbs had failed to destroy the essence of Bosnia-Herzegovina, they caused immense collateral damage to Western credibility and institutions. The UN Security Council, while paying lip service to the inviolability of borders, found a legalistic excuse for ignoring the bedrock principle of international life as embedded in the UN charter: the right to self-defense. The United States recognized Bosnia's territorial integrity and then acquiesced in successive plans to dismantle the republic. Europe ignored the principles of the Conference on Security and Cooperation in Europe, such as inadmissibility of conquest, principles that helped win the Cold War. NATO did its best to patch the differences between Greece and Turkey, but its paralysis prompted questions in the U.S. Congress over the point of a costly mechanism to ensure European security if it cannot stop a small war on its doorstep. The European Community proved itself to be a paper tiger. The "hour of Europe" that peaked in the "great day for the Balkans" dissolved into a sorry moment for Western civilization.

The Bosnia war may have dispelled some illusions. Europeans, rent by national rivalries, remain unable to handle a crisis on their own continent. Lacking the will to use force or the mechanism to agree on its application, the main powers drifted into appeasement and betrayal. "Because America's leadership was not there from the beginning as ... in previous crises ... there was difficulty in galvanizing the nations," Shalikashvili said. "That was a lesson to all of us of the importance of America's leadership and the price we pay when it isn't there."

Although Clinton withdrew from the diplomatic arena, he left the question alive whether Bosnia matters. Christopher's policy statement of February 10 was an eloquent explanation of why it does and the role the United States might play.

"This conflict may be far from our shores, but it is certainly not distant from our concerns. We cannot afford to ignore it," he said.

"The events in the former Yugoslavia raise the question whether a state may address the rights of its minorities by eradicating them to achieve ethnic purity. Bold tyrants and fearful minorities are watching to see whether ethnic cleansing is a policy the world will tolerate. If we hope to promote the spread of freedom, if we hope to encourage the emergence of peaceful ethnic democracies, our answer must be a resounding no."

As if no one had been listening in February, Christopher in a May 26 interview redefined the problem and said the United States could now abandon it. He echoed Neville Chamberlain's famous remark on September 2, 1938, that Britons need not become concerned "because of a quarrel in a faraway country between people of whom we know nothing." In the 1993 rendition by Warren Christopher, Bosnia-Herzegovina was "a humanitarian crisis a long way from home, in the middle of another continent." Americans will not be concerned, he said, because "our actions are proportionate to what our responsibilities are. We can't do it all.

We have to measure our ability to act in the interests of the United States but to save our power for those situations which threaten our deepest national interests."

A vision of a world order based on universal values had succumbed, because of domestic political pressures and diplomatic failure, to the paralysis of isolation.

A WITNESS
TO GENOCIDE

AUSTRIA

HUNGARY

SLOVENIA

Zagreb

ROMANIA

CROATIA

Vojvodina

Omarska

Brezovo-Polje

Tuzla

Belgrade

BOSNIA-
HERZEGOVINA

Caparde

Zvornik

Sarajevo

Serbia

YUGOSLAVIA

Foca

Montenegro

Pristina

Kosovo

Skopje

A d r i a t i c   S e a

MACEDONIA

ITALY

ALBANIA

GREECE

0   MILES   225

Newsday / Fredrick Bus.

Yugoslavs "Need West's Intervention"

Belgrade, Yugoslavia, November 21, 1991

When Yugoslavia erupted into violence in June 1991, the Bush administration dumped the problem in the lap of the European Community and, after ruling out any Western military intervention, stepped offstage. Five months later, EC mediators, their hands tied, have watched helplessly while as many as 10,000 people died and 400,000 were made homeless in the attack on breakaway Croatia by Serbia and the Serb-led federal army.

Today, in the view of Alija Izetbegovic, the respected moderate leader of the republic of Bosnia-Herzegovina, Yugoslavia is sliding into total war, which can be stopped only by Western military intervention.

As the first major conflict since the end of the Cold War and the collapse of Soviet central power, Yugoslavia is the first test of President George Bush's "new world order." But it may be the harbinger of a new world disorder.

In the view of a German diplomat in Bonn, Europe after five months of mediating without any military backup has proved itself "more or less a paper tiger," and the Bush administration is largely to blame.

"What is the United States doing? You are the only ones who could have stopped this war—with but one aircraft carrier in the Adriatic. If 100 American students are trapped in Grenada, you invade the island," said this diplomat, who asked not to be identified.

Jonathan Eyal of the Royal United Services Institute in London, a military think-tank, agreed that action should have been taken sooner. Intervening, he said, "would be a kind of brinkmanship. But my feeling is that the Serbs will run away quickly if they see the possibility of western intervention." Meanwhile, he said, the EC has "failed to understand the nature of the conflict" or "to put anything together to stop it."

State Department and White House officials say the Yugoslav conflict was treated as an internal dispute for reasons unrelated to its merits. "What we are really worried about is the breakup of the Soviet Union," an administration aide said during the Rome NATO summit. "The fear is that if we support the breakup of Yugoslavia, we will encourage the breakup of the Soviet Union." But Eyal thinks the real motivation for staying out was political, for the administration sees no political gain and a great deal of risk in an intervention.

The main impact of U.S. Yugoslavia policy appears to be in western Europe, where it probably was not intended. In turning the matter over to the Europeans, the United States revived a bitter and emotional rivalry that, like the Yugoslav conflict itself, could be seen as a continuation of World War II. During the war Germany was allied with Croatia. Britain sided with Serbia and, following the Nazi invasion, with the Communist partisans.

But the Europeans, divided among themselves, have treated the conflict evenhandedly, dispensing slaps on the wrist to both sides. After announcing sanctions during the Rome NATO summit with the intent of singling out Serbia, they have been unable to agree on the actual step. They called for a United Nations oil embargo, but the effort seems likely to fizzle.

The EC mediation has degenerated into an embarrassment as the Community's white-suited ceasefire monitors, who are derided as "ice cream vendors," submit to humiliation by the Yugoslav army. The EC issues mild protests, which are ignored. According to analysts such as Eyal, the EC's impotent stance may have been interpreted by the Yugoslav army as a green light for conquest.

2

The examples multiply daily:

Ships of four nations were struck by mortars while traveling the Danube through Yugoslavia near Vukovar in the past two weeks. But there wasn't a peep of protest from the EC over the violation of the right of passage on an international waterway.

EC monitors stood by and counted as the Serbian-dominated army last month expelled 10,000 Croatians, the entire population of the east Croatian town of Ilok, a move that gave the army a better jump-off point to attack Croatia.

As the federal army stepped up shelling and tightened its noose around Dubrovnik, which has a protected UN status as one of the treasures of Western civilization, the EC this past weekend quietly withdrew its small monitoring force.

The dispute within the EC centers now on Germany's demands for the Community to recognize Croatia and its neighbor, Slovenia, both of which declared independence on June 25. Recognition would effectively establish an alliance with western Europe and draw western Europe close to the fighting. But Britain is adamantly opposed to such recognition or any use of force to halt the army's onslaught against Croatia.

Yet there is a substantial body of opinion that holds the war can no longer be contained in Yugoslavia and that sooner or later western Europe will be drawn in. "So many things have happened. So many people have been killed. The Yugoslavs are no longer able to settle it by themselves," said Jochen Thies, a scholar with the German Foreign Policy Association. "And an intervention is better sooner rather than later."

Paving the Way for Recognition

Germans Lead EC in Yugoslav Pact

Bonn, Germany, December 18, 1991

Germany, battling like a heavyweight against most of the European Community, has forced the way open for the entire EC to recognize the breakaway Yugoslav republics of Croatia and Slovenia in less than a month.

The compromise, cobbled together in the middle of the night, as most EC accords are, preserved a semblance of European unity by setting up a procedure under which the 12 member nations could establish relations with new countries that succeed the multinational state in mid-January.

But it is only a semblance, for Chancellor Helmut Kohl said yesterday that Germany will announce recognition tomorrow. Under intense pressure by the United States, the UN Security Council and EC partners such as Britain and France, Germany's only concession was to delay implementation until January 15.

And while the EC partners congratulated themselves on avoiding an open split, there was little joy in Yugoslavia itself because the EC action may well have the opposite effect intended: Rather than ending the bloodbath in Croatia, it may expand the war into the ethnic tinderbox of Bosnia-Herzegovina.

The passion with which Kohl and Foreign Minister Hans-Dietrich Genscher have led the drive for recognition has surprised many observers here, for despite its economic and political prowess, Germany is not well placed to influence a war in progress. Germany is prohibited by its constitution from sending either troops or arms into the crisis area to

4

back up its diplomacy, and Genscher has ruled out interventions in any country Nazi Germany occupied during World War II.

"If you follow Genscher's argument, you cannot go anywhere except Great Britain," noted Jochen Thies, editor of the magazine *Europa Archiv*.

An explanation cited by diplomats is repeated entreaties by Pope John Paul II to Kohl, a Roman Catholic, to come to the aid of Croatia and Slovenia, whose populations are predominantly Catholic. President Franjo Tudjman of Croatia, who declared independence on June 25 without any defense preparations, believes that international recognition will turn the tide. Genscher, who is not Catholic, asked the Pope two weeks ago to try to persuade other Roman Catholic countries, including Ireland, Portugal and Poland, to ensure that Germany was not alone in recognizing Croatia, church sources said.

What is most surprising about German policy is that the normally astute Genscher and Kohl do not seem to have thought about the impact on the ground. When asked to explain the impact, Genscher's spokesmen resort to moralisms and legalisms.

One of the most outspoken critics of German policy is the special UN envoy in the Yugoslav crisis, Cyrus Vance. "If recognition leads Bosnia to declare full and complete autonomy, there will be a grave danger of provoking conflict between the Serbs and the army in Bosnia," the secretary of state in the Carter administration said in an interview.

Bosnia's problem is that leaders of the Serb minority, who comprise about 30 percent of its population, say they will not accept independence and will stay in rump Yugoslavia dominated by Serbia, thereby breaking Bosnia apart. But leaders of the Moslems and Croats, who comprise most of the remaining 70 percent, refuse to join a rump Serbia. Already in the ancient town of Mostar there are nightly explosions as Serbs and Croats attack each other's businesses.

Actually, the accord buys a little time for a mission to Yugoslavia by Vance's deputy, U.S. Ambassador Herbert Okun, to try to arrange a ceasefire and the dispatch of a UN force of 10,000 troops. But it is a question of just how much time. The EC accord requires that any Yugoslav republic seeking international recognition on January 15 must apply by Monday and fulfill a number of conditions including guarantees for the rights of ethnic minorities and respect for international frontiers.

European Recognition
May Spark Wider Conflict

Banja Luka, Yugoslavia, December 22, 1991

West Europe's move to recognize Croatian independence touched off a chain reaction yesterday, splitting the ethnically mixed republic of Bosnia-Herzegovina and threatening a wider and more vicious conflict.

The powder keg republic, where World War I began, was divided in two after militant Bosnian Serbs announced they will split off all territories where Serbs are in a majority and seek international recognition as a new republic. That move is expected to arouse strong resistance from Muslims, Croats and other nationalities who comprise 70 percent of Bosnia's population.

Banja Luka, a pleasant city rebuilt with wide boulevards after a devastating earthquake in 1969, is the likely epicenter for the future turmoil. It is in northern Bosnia and is likely to become the capital of the breakaway Serb republic, although 49 percent of its population are non-Serbs.

There is a prospect for a war of catastrophic proportions. "There could be 200,000 to 300,000 people slaughtered within a few months" in Bosnia, Haris Silajdzic, Bosnian foreign minister and a Muslim, said in a recent interview. Official estimates of the people killed in Croatia by the Serbian-dominated federal army or Serbian irregulars since Croatia declared its independence June 25 are in the 10,000 range.

The European Community provided the trigger for expanding the war by requiring each of Yugoslavia's six republics to declare by tomorrow if it wants recognition as an independent state. On Friday, Bosnia-Herzegovina became the latest to seek recognition, following Slovenia, Croatia and Macedonia. Serbia, claiming the mantle of the Balkan state, says it will not. Montenegro, Serbia's war ally, will decide tomorrow.

The predominantly Eastern Orthodox Serbs, who comprise 31 percent of the population, had repeatedly warned Bosnian president Alija Izetbegovic that if he declared independence, they would secede and ally themselves with Serbia. Yesterday, reacting to Izetbegovic's announcement 24 hours earlier, they carried through on the threat. Izetbegovic, viewed by Western diplomats as the most astute politician in Yugoslavia, was in an impossible position. If he had not opted for independence, the mostly Roman Catholic Croats, who make up 17 percent of the population, threatened to withdraw the Croat-dominated territories and join Croatia.

Muslims, who make up 44 percent of the overall population and live throughout Bosnia, have avoided taking sides.

Izetbegovic, a Muslim, had for months battled to postpone international recognition of Croatia because of the violence it is expected to trigger, and won important allies including the United States and special UN envoy Cyrus Vance. But Germany argued successfully to the European Community that to delay recognition rewarded aggression by Serbs.

Izetbegovic gloomly predicted in a recent interview that Bosnia "will probably be drawn into the conflict sooner or later." If so, "it will be total war," and "only an international intervention could prevent this catastrophe," he said. He favors sending a UN peacekeeping force to Bosnia and Croatia, something favored by the United Nations and the European Community. But Bosnian Serbs have flatly rejected such a force.

Banja Luka, a city of 200,000, is at the heart of the dispute. Its population, 51 percent Serb, elected to office radical Serb nationalists, who have already taken all the preliminary steps toward annexing to Serbia proper areas where Serbs are in the majority. They have proclaimed Banja Luka the capital of the so-called Bosnian "Krajina" (pronounced Kray-eena) or border zone.

Predrag Radic, the city council president, received a reporter recently to discuss the Serb plan for dismantling Bosnia. Over coffee and cognac he handed over a color-coded map. Serbs make up less than a third of the population of Bosnia, but according to his map would claim half to two-thirds of its land. Isn't this map a formula for total war?

"It need not occur if the politicians are clever," Radic said. The Serbs would slice off Bosnian Krajina, a large chunk of territory shaped like a boar's head, and connect it with a sickle-shaped slice of Croatia, which Serbia has just recognized as a new republic, to create a new republic called Krajina. It would be the third biggest Yugoslav republic. Also marked are other Serb-led sectors of Bosnia that would secede following a Bosnian declaration of independence.

To link Krajina with Serbia, the maps show two corridors: one proceeding east from Banja Luka toward Serbia, the other a north-south corridor along Croatia's eastern border needed for road and communications connections. That is where the federal army is currently fighting for territory.

Banja Luka, under council president Radic, also provides a glimpse of the link forged between Serb nationalists and the army, which is enabling the Serbs to harness the army to their goal of territorial expansion. According to Radic, the leaders of the Krajina no longer observe Bosnian laws when they conflict with "Yugoslav" laws. Full military mobilization, ruled out by the Bosnian state leadership, is being observed in Bosnian Krajina. "I get faxes every day from the Bosnian defense minister telling me not to support the mobilization, but I ignore them," Radic said, holding up the latest one. Even before the declaration of independence, he said, he planned to withhold taxes from the republican authorities.

The army has a seemingly endless supply of firepower but is crippled by desertions and draft evasion, while the Bosnian Serbs offer motivated troops for the front line and clear political goals for their deployment. Among other things, the ethnic Serbian leadership here has asked the army to protect them from alleged threats by other nationalities. For its part, the federal army's Banja Luka Corps, heavily reliant on Bosnian Serbs, has punched a 15-mile-wide corridor through the heart of Croatia. If extended, as the nationalists project, it will split Croatia in two.

While war has not yet come to Banja Luka, the city is ever closer to the front. Bosanska Gradiska, just 30 miles north, the marshaling point for army convoys, is under constant fire from Croatians trying to cut army lines. There is shooting at night here as well, but mainly by off-duty reserve army troops after drinking bouts. The atmosphere is something out of the Wild West.

"Nobody calls the police because they won't come," said Ibro Tabakovic, a former university rector. "There are too many armed people in town." Thousands of Serbian refugees who had lived in Croatia have flooded the town, straining its resources to the limit.

There are many ways the war could start in Bosnia. After a lull of several weeks, the Banja Luka command brought in several thousand troops, suggesting that another major offensive is in preparation against Croatia, and it is not inconceivable that Croatian forces, if strengthened, would launch punitive raids into Bosnia. At the same time it seems unlikely that an independent Bosnia would allow federal army troops beholden to Serbia to remain here. But there is no clear way to get them to leave, and if they stay in the predominantly Serb territories after they secede from Bosnia, they in effect ensure their secession.

The war in Croatia ended in an uneasy truce early in January 1993, and following negotiations with Croatia, Serbia and the self-styled autonomous Serb region of Krajina by UN mediator Cyrus Vance, the UN Security Council voted February 21 to send nearly 14,000 peacekeeping troops to Croatia. Meanwhile, at the recommendation of a European Community study group headed by French jurist Robert Badinter, Bosnia-Herzegovina scheduled a referendum on its independence for February 29 and March 1.

Bosnia Erupts after Vote
for Independence

Sarajevo, Yugoslavia, March 3, 1992

Ethnic Serbs opposed to independence for the Yugoslav republic of Bosnia-Herzegovina seized control of all roads into the capital yesterday, pushing the multinational region to the brink of civil war.

For nearly 24 hours the city of 600,000 that hosted the 1984 winter Olympics echoed to volleys of small-arms fire and explosions. Four people died and at least eight were injured, including a man and woman fired on during a pro-independence march down a central boulevard, police said. The crowd chanted "Down with the barricades, we are unarmed" and "We love Bosnia" when shots rang out from the direction of the Serbs' barricades.

Even after an agreement between the Muslim-led Bosnian government and the leading Serbian party to end the siege, firing continued into the night, but several of the main blockades were removed.

The blockade began just hours after a referendum in which Muslims and Roman Catholic Croats, who together constitute 60 percent of the 4.3 million Bosnians, voted overwhelmingly to secede from Yugoslavia. Serbs had boycotted the vote, and in what appeared to be a well-planned operation, Serb gunmen wearing ski masks commandeered trucks, buses and streetcars to set up barricades, while others took up positions as snipers.

"We are not going to accept an independent Bosnia-Herzegovina," said Radovan Karadzic, a Serbian party leader, yesterday midway through the siege. And if the majority of Bosnians insisted on independence, "I am afraid we could not avoid an inter-ethnic war," he said. "Let this be a warning."

Karadzic added that ethnic conflict in the republic would make Northern Ireland look like "a seaside holiday." But Bosnian foreign minister Haris Silajdzic said he expected automatic recognition from the European Community, which had demanded the referendum as proof of support in Bosnia for independence. "It is the will of the citizens that we are an independent and sovereign state now," he said in a comment on the unofficial results.

The blockade most directly affected residents of the predominantly Muslim historic quarter, but those trapped included the entire Bosnian government, more than 100 foreign observers who came to monitor the referendum and at least 500 reporters.

"We got in past the barricades this morning, but they wouldn't let us out," said Colm Doyle, chief of the European Community peace-monitoring mission. But later the Serbs agreed to allow two busloads of foreign observers to depart for Sarajevo airport.

The siege prompted a countermove by Muslims, who set up barricades around Serb districts of the city. And as shooting continued through the day in and around the old city, young Muslims marched on the city hall and demanded weapons to defend themselves. "Give me your gun. I will take three Chetniks [Serb extremists] hostage," said one young unarmed man in the crowd to a man in dark glasses wearing a green beret and carrying a semiautomatic weapon.

"You allowed the guns to be taken away," said another, referring to the disarming of the Muslim militia by the Yugoslav army last year. City officials refused the demands, but a few hours later most of the men on the otherwise deserted streets appeared to be armed.

Serbs at first said the siege was a response to the shooting of a Serb man waving a Serbian flag in the Muslim quarter of town on Sunday afternoon. But Karadzic's party then laid down a set of demands, making it clear that the shooting was only a pretext.

The United States and the European Community formally recognized Bosnia-Herzegovina, Slovenia and Croatia, on April 7, and Bosnian Serbs declared an independent republic that same day. The Yugoslav federal army or paramilitary forces under its supervision came in from Serbia and seized control of cities and towns on the Bosnian side of the Drina River, which forms the boundary between Serbia and Bosnia-Herzegovina. On April 27, Serbia and tiny Montenegro proclaimed a new Federal Republic of Yugoslavia. At the same time the Serb-dominated Yugoslav army announced its withdrawal from Bosnia—in fact, concentrated its forces in areas dominated by the Serb minority, changed uniforms, and left its weapons in the hands of the Bosnian Serbs. On May 1 the Army began shelling the capital around the clock. Ten days later, on May 11 and 12, in protest, the European Community and the United States withdrew their ambassadors from Belgrade, the Serbian capital.

Serb Author Lit Balkan Powder Keg

Belgrade, Yugoslavia, June 28, 1992

As the world looks on in anguish, Serbian forces are systematically destroying Sarajevo, and Serb irregulars are "cleansing" Bosnian villages of Muslim inhabitants, turning a tourist showplace into a charnel house.

From afar it may seem incomprehensible, but for anyone familiar with the works of Serbia's most popular writer, the revival of Dark Ages primitivism in the Balkans comes as no surprise. The blueprint is in the novels and political essays of Dobrica Cosic, who on June 15 became president of Yugoslavia's rump federation. Cosic, 71, styles himself the "father of his people." His writing portrays Serbia as the superior Slav nation in the Balkans, glorifying its victories in war while regretting that Serbs always lose the peace. Cosic revived the expansionist slogan of the nineteenth century: All Serbs in one state.

But Cosic (whose name is pronounced DAW-brit-sa CHAW-sitch) went beyond promoting the carving up of other Yugoslav republics. Behind the scenes he also developed a network of extreme nationalists among the Serb minorities in Croatia, Bosnia-Herzegovina and the Albanian-dominated Serbian province of Kosovo who have used force to try to carry out his program.

Cosic is the spiritual father of Slobodan Milosevic, the Serbian strongman, and one of his protégés runs Belgrade television, Milosevic's instrument for whipping up nationalist passions.

"If you could measure it in percentage terms, he has been the most influential Serb over the last 15 to 20 years," commented Alexander Tijanic, a newspaper editor who has closely followed Cosic's career.

What prompted Cosic to take on the ceremonial role as president of the federation of Serbia and Montenegro is unclear. The two states are all that remain of Yugoslavia after the four other former republics declared their independence over Serbia's violent objection. The remains of the Yugoslavian army and Serbian irregulars have been waging war for a year against the separatists, culminating in the siege of Sarajevo, which had been the perfect example of a multiethnic city.

With inflation climbing at 4 percent a day, the war economy in near-ruins and international economic sanctions starting to bite, domestic opposition to Milosevic is building, and the threat of civil war in Serbia is growing. Milosevic is under attack by some nationalists who believe he has lost the war, while a growing opposition, centering around students at Belgrade University, is attacking him because he began it. They are mounting what they hope will be a major rally today to demand Milosevic's resignation.

Many in the opposition think Cosic will push Milosevic aside. "Serbia has to close its eyes and hold its nose in the hope that Dr. Frankenstein will succeed in stopping his monster," the newsweekly *Vreme* said last week.

Cosic personifies a little-known aspect of the baffling conflict that began a year ago with the secession of Slovenia and Croatia from the former multinational state. Milosevic is widely blamed for the bloodbath in Croatia and the wanton destruction in Bosnia; and the men firing on Sarajevo apartment houses may be unlettered peasants, but the program came largely from Cosic, and the seal of approval came from scholars and writers at the once-prestigious Serbian Academy of Arts and Sciences.

Once a close associate of the late president Josip Broz Tito and a member of the Serbian Communist Party Central Committee, Cosic broke with the party over Serbian nationalism. As communism weakened with the death of Tito in 1981, Cosic stood out as an example of a communist-turned-nationalist who gained influence and wealth in the process.

Serbia today is a mystery to outsiders. Belgrade, the capital, has a modestly prosperous appearance, and educated Serbs have charmed more than a generation of diplomats and journalists into thinking this was a Western country-in-waiting. Appearances give no clue to the descent into primitivism among a people who have a proud, if bloodstained, history of fighting for their independence and who were on the Allied side in both world wars. Serbia is going full steam backward.

A good deal of the reason lies in Tito's preference for suppressing national hatreds and his failure to create a market economy and stable political institutions. Those who know Serbia well, however, cite as a decisive factor the corruption of the educated elite.

"Our intellectuals have always been paid. In the Tito era they were sitting in the Communist Party Central Committee or parliament," said Latinka Perovic, a historian and senior Serbian party official purged by Tito for pro-Western policies. "The whole of cultural life was turned over to them. This compromised both the regime and the intellectuals. In fact, they participated in power. If they now put everything on the national card, it should not be surprising."

Serbia, she said, is not willing to see the truth "about what it has done" in the war. "No one asks how it was possible," she said. "People here are protected from the truth. The only thing that surprises me is the attitude of our intellectuals toward the suffering of others. They think it all happened to someone else."

Cosic's extreme nationalism first surfaced in 1968 when he warned a party meeting that Serbs were being suppressed in Kosovo, a southern province inhabited mainly by ethnic

Albanians. If the suppression did not cease, he warned, Serbs would break apart the multinational state by reviving the "old historical goal and national ideal" of uniting "all Serbs in one state."

"There was a shocked silence, and we called a break," recalled Petar Stambolic, then a senior party official. "That was the beginning of the nationalist line in Serbian politics. You can follow a constant thread from that point."

Twenty years later Milosevic, a Communist Party bureaucrat, rode Cosic's themes to power, carrying out a brutal crackdown in Kosovo on the grounds that Serbs were being suppressed there. "I disagree with the description of Milosevic as a nationalist-Bolshevist," said Slavoljub Djukic, biographer of both Cosic and Milosevic. "I see him more as a man without political convictions."

Cosic edited a draft memorandum at the Academy of Sciences in 1986 asserting that Kosovo was "not the only region where the Serb people are under pressure of discrimination" and that Serbian "survival and development" were in question in Croatia as well.

Early last year Cosic slammed Croats as "the strongest destructive force in Yugoslavia and leaders in the anti-Serbian coalition." He reiterated the "Serbian people's historical aim—the unification of all Serbs into one state" and rejected a confederation of republics on the grounds their boundaries were "not legitimate, either historically or legally." Milosevic adopted the line, and a peaceful reorganization of Yugoslavia became impossible.

Last July, as Serb irregulars set up gun positions and began pounding Croatian cities to provoke the war in eastern Croatia, Cosic announced that Yugoslavia had been destroyed, that there was "wild hatred against the Serbian people" and that "pacifist rhetoric is senseless." He called on Serbs to "create their own state on their ethnic territories" and finally "conclude the struggle for liberation and unification that has lasted for two centuries." He praised

Milosevic as the "best Serbian leader" in a half-century. Cosic never went beyond his broad guidelines and withheld comment on the subsequent slaughter. He did not call for the armed Serbian uprising in Bosnia-Herzegovina, but the offensive was implicit in his program to unite all Serbs in one state. Today there is only a modest prospect of Cosic's united Serbian state, and his freedom of action is limited.

Serbs "now have the feeling of being losers," said human rights activist Sonja Liht, who noted the expectation that Kosovo, too, will soon break away. Under growing pressure and with armed paramilitary forces at his call, Milosevic may decide to provoke conflict against his internal opposition in Serbia as well, spelling a devastating civil war.

Cosic is faced with the choice of attempting to oust Milosevic or supporting him as the ship sinks. He is being called on to write a new chapter of Serbia's history, but the titles of his two trilogies sum up the situation he helped to bring about. One is titled *The Time of Death,* and the other, *The Time of Evil.*

❖

Ethnic Cleansing:
Yugoslavs Try to Deport
1,800 Muslims to Hungary

Palic, Yugoslavia, July 3, 1992

In a practice not seen in Europe since the end of World War II, the Serbian-led government of Yugoslavia chartered an 18-car train last week in an attempt to deport the entire population of a Muslim village to Hungary.

Some 1,800 passengers, including 70 mothers carrying infants, were expelled from the east Bosnian village of Kozluk after two armored tanks crashed into the main square and Serb irregulars threatened to blow it up, according to the villagers. They were ordered onto the Hungary-bound train, but only a fraction had travel documents and Hungary refused to admit them. After four days on board, the villagers were brought to a camp for Muslims in Palic, close to the Hungarian border, filling it to three times its capacity.

The incident was the latest twist of cruelty in an already brutal war, foreign officials say, part of a policy by the Serbian-led Yugoslav government to "ethnically cleanse" historically Muslim areas of Bosnia.

Foreign monitors are convinced that Serbian strongman Slobodan Milosevic is backing the use of tanks and terror by Serb militia forces, then deploying the Serbian Red Cross to finish the job. The local Red Cross, which international observers say is operating as an adjunct of the Serbian government, has sent or tried to send at least 7,000 Bosnians out of the country in what United Nations officials view as a violation of international law governing the treatment of refugees.

The deportation train was not an isolated instance, said Ron Redmond, a spokesman for the UN High Commissioner for Refugees in Geneva. The commission views the practice of ethnic cleansing and any action supporting it as "a travesty," he said. The UN commission is preparing a protest to the Yugoslav federation about the deportations, commission officials in Belgrade said.

The Serb-backed assault in Bosnia has created the biggest flood of refugees in Europe since World War II. The UN commission estimated this week that 1.7 million people have lost their homes in the past year: 1.1 million from Bosnia-Herzegovina and 617,000 from Croatia. The number is growing by several thousand a day.

About 204,000 war refugees from Bosnia are in Serbia, about 40,000 of them Muslims and the rest Serbs. The Serbian Red Cross places Serb refugees in private homes or in hotels but, according to Serbian Red Cross officials, it is trying wherever possible to send the Muslims out of the country.

At Bajina Basta, a refugee staging point on the Serbian side of the Drina River, the Red Cross chapter secretary defended the practice. "There are too many dead [Serb] bodies coming across the river. No one who loses a relative is very eager to accommodate those from the other side," said Nada Ivanovic. It was Ivanovic who packed off five busloads of Visegrad refugees, against their wishes, to Macedonia. "They wanted to go there," she said last week. But Abdulahu Osmanagulis, the refugees' unofficial leader, said, "We had no choice."

The Serbian Red Cross director of the Palic camp, where the Muslims on the refugee train were taken, made similar claims. The camp director, who identified herself only as "Nada," said that all the refugees "left their homes voluntarily" and signed papers turning over their property to newly installed Serb authorities in Bosnia. She said at least 5,000 people had been processed through the camp. She insisted on monitoring interviews with ethnic Muslims, intimidating many. Conditions are primitive, and many refugees, the elderly in particular, have nowhere to sit, but they universally denied her claims.

Hadim Kavazovic-Osmanovic, 60, from Zvornik, was sitting on the ground at the camp when the deportation train pulled into the station about a mile away. Like those on the train, he had been terrorized by Serbian militia forces who forced him to flee his homeland.

"We were forced to leave. We were under threat," he said. "They were killing people during the night. Someone came from the local government and said it was better to leave."

"When we crossed the bridge into Serbia, the border officials told us we could enter but not come back," said Camila Mehmedbegovic, 59, another expellee from Zvornik. Two other women from the town said they had deeded their houses, their land and all the property to the Serbian army.

Those on the deportation train told a similar tale. Residents of Kozluk, a town of 5,000 north of Zvornik, like Visegrad, in the Drina River Valley, described a nightmare that began when Serbs seized control of the area in April. They installed new leaders, who about a month ago summarily dismissed Muslims from their jobs. Food and medicine deliveries stopped, and after Serb irregulars robbed and burned down houses and raped several women, the Muslims offered to depart. Last Thursday two tanks rolled into the village.

"They told us they could no longer assure us protection," said Mulaibisevic Mohmedalisa, 35. "They said this was part of an ethnically pure Serbian region, and it was inconvenient to have a Muslim village at a key road junction."

The remaining residents of Kozluk were taken by bus to Sabac in northern Serbia, where the special train was waiting for them, and sent to the Hungarian border.

"The whole thing was arranged in advance," said Judith Kumin, the UN High Commission on Refugees representative in Belgrade, the Serbian capital. Kumin said there was no way the UN relief agency, with a staff of 85 for all the former Yugoslav republics and in the context of a refugee problem that is exploding "exponentially," could provide staff to protect the rights of refugees at the Palic camp.

"The River Took Him"

Miratovac, Yugoslavia, July 3, 1992

Hasnija Pjeva witnessed the execution of her husband, Nenad, from the terrace of her house outside Visegrad.

It was 7:30 A.M., June 24, and Nenad was returning from his overnight factory shift when the armed men in Serbian paramilitary uniforms spotted him. Nenad started running to the nearby riverbank, but the irregulars shot him dead on the spot. They dragged the corpse onto the bridge, then threw it into the green water of the Drina.

"I didn't bury him," Hasnija said of her husband two days later, tears welling in her eyes. "The river took him away."

Abdulahu Osmanagulis was at his home in Visegrad, a virtual prisoner since Serb forces seized the predominantly Muslim town three months before. They burned down the two ancient mosques and roamed the streets, firing small arms day and night. Early last week three of his neighbors were shot in their home.

"The bodies were just left lying there in the courtyard," Osmanagulis said. He knew it was time to get out of his house.

Emina Hodzic's husband was abducted one noon, her son that same evening. Mediha Tira's husband was taken away by men with blackened faces.

The killings all happened last week in the Bosnian town whose Turkish-built "bridge on the Drina" was immortalized by Yugoslavian novelist Ivo Andric. There are now two bridges, and after last week's events, both will find their place in the literature of war atrocities.

Except for an unknown but apparently small number who

escaped, all the able-bodied Muslim men and youths of Visegrad who had not fled the occupiers were shot, according to a dozen survivors.

"Most of the executions were committed on the bridge. Their bodies were thrown into the river," said Osmanagulis, 73, the unofficial leader of the survivors. It appears that dozens were executed, perhaps hundreds. No one knows exactly.

"If the Drina River could only speak, it would say how many dead were taken away," said Hasnija Pjeva.

Visegrad (pronounced VEE-shih-grad), with a population of about 30,000, is one of a number of towns where Serb forces carried out "ethnic cleansing" of Muslims in the past two weeks, according to the Bosnian government.

"There was chaos in Visegrad. Everything was burned, looted and destroyed," said a Visegrad expellee, 43, who spoke of the terrible events over coffee in the Miratovac cafe but would give neither his name nor his profession. He escaped only because he was an invalid with a gangrenous leg.

The survivors of the massacre are the old, the infirm, the women and the children. They are traumatized by what they witnessed, barely able to speak or to control their emotions. Two of the women had been raped, Osmanagulis said. But the heartbreak was compounded by the humiliation they endured at the hands of the local Serbian Red Cross.

Against their wishes, 280 people were shipped in a convoy of five buses across Serbia, the principal state in the new Yugoslavia, to Macedonia, a breakaway state, a journey of about 275 miles. The Serbian Red Cross gave them food and clothes but insisted they sign papers saying they had been well treated and wanted to go to Macedonia.

"We all wanted to go to Kosovo or Sandzak," two mainly Muslim areas of southern Serbia, said Osmanagulis, "but they directed us exclusively to Macedonia. There was no other choice."

He carried a paper requesting that the Macedonian border authorities provide passports and admit the entire group. But Macedonia, which has more than 30,000 Bosnian refugees but has yet to be recognized by Western countries or to receive any real assistance, has stopped accepting any refugees, particularly Muslims, due to substantial problems with its own Muslim minority, according to Mira Jankovska, a government spokeswoman in Skopje.

And so the Macedonians refused to allow the survivors of the Visegrad massacre to cross the border. It was 4 A.M.

Osmanagulis conferred with the drivers, and they agreed that everyone should disembark and try to enter on foot, but the Macedonian police turned them away. "I ran back to the buses and everyone followed, but when the drivers saw us, they turned the buses around and left," he said.

For 16 hours on June 25 the survivors found themselves stranded in a no-man's-land on an international highway without food, water, shelter or assistance, abandoned by the Red Cross and welcomed nowhere. Fifteen of them were over 80, and there were at least as many children under the age of 2. They stood and sat from 4 A.M. until 8 P.M., through the hot midday sun and a fierce summer rainstorm.

Albanian Muslims in this impoverished farm village in southern Serbia, about a 20-minute drive from the border crossing, brought bread, water and tomatoes. Then in the evening they arrived with tractors and taxis and took them to a small mosque here. On the advice of a local doctor who feared the spread of disease, the survivors were moved to private homes two days later.

"If the people of the village hadn't helped us, half of us would be dead of starvation or illness," said Osmanagulis. One woman, 92, died after the ordeal. She was buried Sunday.

Now the survivors of Visegrad sit in this village at the end of a potholed dirt road, sleeping on the floors and couches of its simple houses, caught between the hostility of Serbia and Macedonia, unattended by any refugee organization, unable even to contact anyone outside, for there is no telephone.

"We have a saying," said Osmanagulis, summing up their plight: "The sky is too high, and the ground is too hard."

Prisoners of Serbia's War

Tales of Hunger, Torture at Camp in North Bosnia

Manjaca, Bosnia-Herzegovina, July 19, 1992

Heads bowed and hands clasped behind their backs, the Muslim prisoners lined up before their Serb captors. One by one they sat on the metal stool and then knelt to have their heads shaved.

An order was given that could not be heard from 200 yards away, and each group of 20 then returned on the double to the sheds in which they lived in near-darkness. Guards at the entry swung their rubber truncheons as if in anticipation of beatings to come.

The scene was a harrowing, if unintended, demonstration to a visiting reporter of the indignities that the all-powerful Serbian army in Bosnia metes out daily to Muslims and Croats in the ethnic cleansing of all other nationalities in territories it conquers.

The army calls Manjaca a prisoner-of-war camp. But inside the vast sheds, where this reporter was forbidden to go, beatings and torture are an integral part of the daily regime, according to just-released Muslim prisoners. At least three prisoners died in the past month, they said.

The prisoners sleep on stone floors with only ferns as mattresses and one blanket for four men or youths. Eight share a space equivalent to a horse stall. They have a shower every two weeks, and most are still wearing the clothes they arrived in six weeks ago.

The occasion for the Tuesday visit to Manjaca, the first by any Western reporter, was that the International Red Cross was performing its first inspection of the camp that same day.

"We are concealing nothing," Col. Milutin Vuketic, the deputy commander of the army's Krajina corps, told *Newsday* at his nearby headquarters as he kept the Red Cross staff waiting. But the army turned down *Newsday*'s request for a tour, offering instead interviews with eight hand-picked prisoners and a camp doctor. Armed guards monitored each conversation, army interviewers asked most of the questions, and an army television team recorded the scene. None of the prisoners interviewed under those conditions criticized the camp's regime, but former prisoners interviewed away from the camp described it as a place where beatings were routine.

The eight interviewees were marched in formation into a small plaza near the camp entrance. Their heads were bowed and their hands clasped behind their backs as they entered. They had been given prison uniforms but wore the shoes they came with, mostly without laces. All looked pale, weary and under duress.

Everything here is good, considering the conditions, said V., one of the prisoners, as guards monitored his words. There is food and accommodation. Everything is fine.

Manjaca (pronounced MAHN-ya-tcha) is one of a string of new detention facilities; an American embassy official in Belgrade routinely refers to them as concentration camps. It is another example of the human-rights abuses now exploding to a dimension unseen in Europe since the Nazi Third Reich.

Witnesses in Banja Luka, Zagreb and other locations describe executions, mass deportations in closed freight cars, forced marches and a regime of starvation and abandonment to the elements.

Manjaca is operated by the army, which still maintains a certain discipline among its troops. Leaders of the principal Muslim charitable organization and political party call it a first-class hotel compared with the nightmarish accounts they have heard about the camps run by local police in municipalities of northern Bosnia.

The camp is in hilly country about 15 miles south of Banja Luka, the second largest city in the new republic and the principal stronghold of Serb militants. Just below the site is an enormous army base bristling with tanks, rockets and other military equipment. A hand-painted sign at the edge of the camp warns: DO NOT ENTER, PENALTY OF DEATH.

With its multiple perimeters of barbed-wire fence, its newly dug minefields and its guard posts, the former army exercise grounds have the appearance of a Stalag 17 or the former East-West German border. There are hundreds of armed police and military guards for the estimated 3,000 prisoners, and the watchmen use German shepherd dogs as they patrol the grounds. As the Red Cross delegation arrived last week, prisoners were out on the grounds building what appeared to be another perimeter fence.

Yet it was by no means clear that the detainees were really prisoners of war, for a good many say they did not even take up arms against the Serbs who attacked their towns. Two of the eight prisoners presented for interviews said they were not sure why they had been brought to the camp, and two others said they had legally registered guns, which they turned over as demanded by the Serb conquerors of their villages.

S., a Croat, said he had been captured unarmed while delivering food to the defenders of his village, Mile kod Jelice, when it came under Serb attack one month ago. V., a Muslim, said that the Muslim community in his town, Skucana Vakuf, had surrendered to the Serbs and that he was not sure why he was detained. "Even I don't know," he said. "I am wondering." Both men appeared to be in their mid-thirties. (The names of sources are not used in this story to protect them in the dangerous circumstances in which they are living.)

According to a leader of Merhamet, a respected Muslim charitable organization in Banja Luka, most people at Manjaca have no connection with the military clashes.

Former prisoners at Manjaca, released last week, also said that only a few of those at the camp ever fought the Serbs. The camp may in fact have been set up for another purpose—to collect hostages for an exchange. Banja Luka's mayor, Predrag Radic, said the Serbs had offered to exchange Manjaca prisoners for Serb POWs being held by Croats and Muslims.

But if these were not fighters, their arbitrary and brutal treatment during transport to the camp and imprisonment there seem almost inexplicable.

"They took us from our homes on May 27," said S., a 17-year-old Muslim from the town of Kljuc. "There was no fighting. They said we would receive a paper, but we never got anything." First taken to Sanski Most and held for 12 days, he, his father, grandfather and brother were then sent in a convoy of six covered trucks, each packed with 150 or more people, to Manjaca.

Eighteen people died on the way, he said. "I saw the pile of bodies after the trip. There was just not enough air to breathe. They died of asphyxiation."

The young man, interviewed at the mosque in Banja Luka where the army dumped 105 prisoners last week, asked not to be identified out of fear for the rest of his family, including his father who is still at Manjaca.

K., a 17-year-old from Sanica Gornja, said he was arrested May 29 when army soldiers invaded the largely Muslim village. "No bullet was fired from the Muslim side, but the Serbs shot and killed people," he said. His uncle, who was in possession of a hunter's carbine rifle, was executed in front of his house, he said. His father was taken away and executed; K. said he learned this after being released from the prison.

He and other able-bodied men from his village were taken in trucks to Kljuc. There they were interrogated and beaten with steel cables, nightsticks, gun butts and rubber truncheons, he said. "There were 300 people at the school, and over nine days we got only two sandwiches to eat," he said.

But that was only the prelude for the greater ordeal. They were taken 20 miles by bus to the town of Sitnice and on disembarking had to run a 150-yard gauntlet of guards who beat them. Yugoslav Communists used the practice at the Goli Otok concentration camp shortly after World War II, and it is nicknamed "hot rabbit." "It was impossible to get from one end to the other in less than five minutes," K. said. After being held at Sitnice for a week, they were forced to walk another 20 miles to Manjaca. "For two days we had nothing to eat. We were given one glass of water. Anyone who could not walk was beaten," he said.

They reached the camp, exhausted, on June 7. "You only got two deciliters [a few ounces] of water, enough to wet your lips every other day. There were some days without any bread," K. recalled.

Every second day camp guards beat him in the evening, after the prisoners had gone to bed. Guards would walk past the stalls and read out about 10 names. Prisoners would follow them to a small room near the kitchen, and each would be beaten for 20 minutes to a half-hour.

"We were beaten until we fell over. It was best to stay up as long as you could. It was easier to take body blows than to be kicked," K. said. One prisoner got the nickname "Rubber Man" because he never let himself be knocked down.

Answering questions in the camp last week, the camp doctor, a Muslim and a prisoner himself, said there had been no deaths there except for one person who died of a heart attack. But K. said two men, a 30-year-old Croat and a 26-year-old Muslim, had died in the past month of mistreatment.

On the afternoon that the doctor addressed visitors, Mirsad Mesenovic, a 27-year-old man from Blagoje, was buried in nearby Banja Luka. Mesenovic had been shot in the spine and was taken to Manjaca, but according to K. and other newly released prisoners, he was given only first aid. He was released from camp on July 11 and died the next day in Banja Luka.

Many prisoners had broken ribs and other injuries, but no one went to the doctor, fearing more beatings, he said.

When they were released, K. and his fellow prisoners had no papers or documents. They were taken to Banja Luka and deposited at a Muslim mosque. According to the official local newspaper, *Banja Luka Glas,* they are permitted to walk around the town but cannot return to their homes in northern Bosnia.

They have no personal documents, nor do they expect to see them again. In the ultimate expression of the camp leadership's contempt for its prisoners, guards dumped all the prisoners' personal papers—passports, driver's licenses, letters, prescriptions, even money—into two large cardboard boxes in the doctor's office. There they remain.

"There Is No Food, There Is No Air'"

Banja Luka, Bosnia-Herzegovina, July 19, 1992

The camp is an open pit where only a third of the prisoners have shelter from the elements and most have to stand in mud, according to a witness. Six to 10 people die daily.

"The corpses pile up. There is no food. There is no air to breathe. No medical care. Even the grass around the pit has been completely clawed away," said an official of Merhamet, the Muslim relief agency, who received the account last week. "Our hair stood up when we heard the report."

There are mounting indications that Omarska, a town near this capital of Serb-conquered north Bosnia, houses a death camp where Serb authorities, with the backing of the army, have taken thousands of Muslims. Hepatitis is reportedly epidemic, and other diseases are spreading rapidly. The witness quoted the camp commander as warning the inmates that they will never leave it alive. The reports could not be independently confirmed.

Unlike Manjaca, a camp that has been known to international relief agencies since it was used by the Yugoslav army to house prisoners during its war against Croatia last year, almost nothing definitive is known about Omarska or a dozen other detention camps run by the local police across northern Bosnia. The International Red Cross has placed Omarska on a list of camps it intends to visit but has not yet formally asked permission to do so.

Interviews with refugees from this area of northern Bosnia suggest that at least some detainees at Omarska took up arms and fought the army when it attacked their towns and villages. Thus, unlike Manjaca, Omarska may be a genuine prisoner-of-war camp

"What you saw at Manjaca is a class A hotel compared with the others," said the Merhamet official, whose name is not being used for his protection. He said civil and military authorities have repeatedly rebuffed Merhamet's requests to send a delegation or food to the camp. Part of the problem is that no authority will state who actually runs the camp. "I guarantee you, you will never find out who is responsible for it," the Merhamet official said.

An official with the Muslim political party, SDA, estimated that 30,000 Muslims and Croats are being held in camps in the region around Banja Luka. Other camps are being used for other ethnic groups. Camps also have been set up for Serbs who refuse to join the mandatory military mobilization.

Former prisoners at Manjaca speak of a second camp nearby where young Serbs were taken from Banja Luka. "We understand there are 700 Serbs there. We could hear them, like starving wolves, at night," said K., a 17-year-old who was released from Manjaca a little over a week ago.

Military authorities and the local Red Cross acknowledged the existence of a camp at Omarska but rebuffed requests to visit it. "There are places where Muslim extremists have been gathered," said Maj. Milovan Milutinovic, the spokesman for the former Yugoslav army which has renamed itself the Serbian Army of Bosnia. "But I think they have already been moved."

A local Red Cross official said he knew of "no civilians" in Omarska.

The SDA official said the military had rejected all requests for visits on the grounds that Omarska is "in a high-risk zone." He noted that a railroad runs through Omarska and that trains have operated regularly.

"Like Auschwitz"

Serbs Pack Muslims into Freight Cars

Banja Luka, Bosnia-Herzegovina, July 21, 1992

In their zeal to "cleanse" northern Bosnia of its Muslims and Croats, Serbs who seized control of the region have deported thousands of unarmed civilians in sealed freight trains in the past month. Hundreds of women, children and old people have been packed into each freight car for sweltering journeys lasting three or more days into central Bosnia, according to refugees who survived the ordeal.

"There was no food, no water and no fresh air," said Began Fazlic. "There was no toilet, just holes in the floor" that piled high with excrement. An unknown number of people, particularly children and the aged, have died in the deportations, according to first-person accounts.

"You could only see the hands of the people in the tiny ventilation holes," said an official of the SDA, the Muslim political party, who saw the first two trains. "But we were not allowed to come close. It was like Jews being deported to Auschwitz."

Today, according to Muslim community leaders, there are no Muslims left in any of the major towns of northwest Bosnia where they had made up as much as 90 percent of the population.

The method of deportation was confirmed by Stojan Zupljanin, the police chief in Banja Luka, Bosnia-Herzegovina's second largest city and the stronghold of ethnic Serbs in Bosnia. "We arranged 'safe transportation'" for Muslims who wanted to emigrate, he said.

With more than a million Bosnians made homeless by the

Serb assault, passenger trains full of deportees are waiting at the borders of the former Yugoslavia for willing host countries. But movements within northern Bosnia have been almost exclusively in sealed freight trains, according to Muslim officials here.

According to eyewitnesses, the first two trains, carrying about 4,000 deportees from the town of Kozarac, passed through Banja Luka around June 12. Some were transported in passenger cars, but the majority rode in cattle cars.

"Even the people in the passenger cars looked exhausted and were in terrible shape. But the guards allowed no one to communicate with them," said an official of Merhamet, the respected Muslim charity in Banja Luka, who also witnessed the first trains. (Both the Merhamet and SDA sources are now in physical danger, and their names are not being used.)

Since the trains around June 12, according to Muslim officials, freight trains packed with deportees have moved through Banja Luka regularly but after a nighttime curfew when no citizen is allowed near the station.

A spokeswoman for the International Red Cross said last week that the organization had heard rumors of deportations in sealed freight cars but had been unable to establish any definitive facts.

Police chief Zupljanin painted a rosy picture of the deportation, suggesting that the elderly men, the mothers with infants and the small children had in fact asked to be deported in a way that violates international conventions protecting civilians in wartime. Zupljanin asserted that the trains had been organized because "a certain number of [Muslim and Croat] citizens had expressed their wish to move to central Bosnia." He implied that the refugees were happy to be carried in cattle cars. "None of the refugees asked for first-class carriages," he said. "None of them said, 'If you don't have a passenger train, I wouldn't go.' Anything is better than walking." He indicated that the alternative was a forced march of up to 100 miles.

Asked why police would not allow Muslim volunteers to provide food and water to the refugees, Zupljanin said only: "It was a safety measure."

In fact, local Serbs, who seized power and declared autonomy last spring without consulting Muslims and Croats in the region, drove them at gunpoint out of the villages and towns where their families had lived for centuries, many refugees say. The Muslims were in the way of a strategic goal that extreme Serbian nationalists have promoted for years: the creation of a corridor between the republic of Serbia and Krajina, an isolated pocket of Serbs in the middle of Croatia. Banja Luka's mayor, Predrag Radic, told *Newsday* last November that Serbs intended to establish a secure corridor in northern Bosnia linking the two Serb communities. Thanks to an enormous military assault by the Yugoslav army, that corridor is now a fact, the central military achievement of three months of war.

To implement Serbian strategy, refugees from throughout northern Bosnia and Muslim officials in Banja Luka said the Serb-controlled army launched direct assaults using artillery, mortar and tanks against nearly every town or large village.

In mid-May and early June local police and militias rounded up non-Serbs, transported them in trucks and buses to sports halls, schools and stadiums and then ordered them aboard the freight trains. The police chief confirmed that two freight trains carrying expellees passed through Banja Luka about a month ago, but he said he could not recall any subsequent movements. A local Red Cross official said he was aware of other evacuations by trains involving Muslims and Croats from the towns of Bosanski Novi and Prijedor.

According to Merhamet and the SDA, through the middle of last week there were at least 10 trains in the past month, with a total of 100 cars. They estimated that 20,000 people were deported in this manner.

"A friend of mine went to the station to look for relatives on the train," said a longtime resident of Banja Luka who could be endangered by the publication of his name. "She couldn't find them, but she found some of their neighbors. She came back sobbing. She said the people looked pale and exhausted and afraid. Some were still dressed in their nightgowns."

The world community and international relief groups have condemned "ethnic cleansing" as a barbarous practice that also has produced Europe's largest refugee flood since World War II. But little was known of the workings of the process, in particular the internal deportations, because access to northern Bosnia had been curtailed until 10 days ago as the army conducted its clearing operation.

During a three-day visit to Banja Luka by a *Newsday* reporter and a freelance photographer, the army declined to provide logistical support or guarantee safety for any trips other than those organized by the command. But through contacts with political parties and governmental and charitable institutions, it was possible to learn at least the outlines of the deportation process.

The authorities made use of the only rail line in northern Bosnia to deport refugees from northwest Bosnia. The principal destination appears to be the central Bosnia region surrounding Zenica, which after the Serb-led blitzkrieg is one of the few remaining Muslim-controlled areas in the entire republic. Despite checks with local officials in several towns on the route, there is no indication that the refugees arrived in Zenica except for the first two trains a month ago. It is not known where the deportees on other trains were taken.

"We had to ask from all around for trains. We were doing our best," said Zupljanin. But "best" is a matter of definition. The regional Red Cross official disclosed that on one occasion, on or around June 18, a freight train filled with deportees was sent into a battle zone and was left there until he negotiated safe passage with his Croat and Muslim counterparts.

"We only get involved in these evacuations when passage

is closed," said Miroslav Djekic, secretary of the regional Red Cross. "We made contact with the Red Cross on the other side of the front lines and asked them to provide safe passage. After an agreed ceasefire, the train proceeded and the refugees somehow made their way out of Bosnia and into Croatia," he said.

Although the Red Cross is almost always involved in movements of civilians in war zones in civil and international-al wars, Djekic said the Serb-controlled government of this region, known as Bosnian Krajina, had decided to restrict its role to cases where safe passage must be negotiated through a conflict zone. And it founded a parallel organization with the innocuous name Center for the Reception of Refugees; it handles all the evacuations from northern Bosnia.

The center takes shortcuts, to judge from another account that originated with refugees who had escaped from a deportation train and returned to Banja Luka. According to a source who heard it from the refugees, the deportees trav-eled for four days and nights without food or water when their train halted in the middle of a clearing. There the doors to the freight cars were opened, and the passengers were told, "Get out and walk to the Muslim region." During the all-night walk of about 15 miles to the town of Maglaj, two women gave birth and one old man died. "They had to dig the grave by hand," the source said.

Seska Stanojlovic contributed to this story.

Muslims Relate Atrocities

Zagreb, Croatia, July 21, 1992

When he emerged from a sealed freight car after three days, Began Fazlic was left with memories of the torture he had witnessed during the Serbian conquest of his native town of Kozarac.

On May 17, after Serbian forces entered the town, Fazlic, other elderly residents, women and children were taken to the nearby village of Trnopolje. They spent two weeks in a detention center set up inside a sports hall. The able-bodied men and youths of Kozarac, including one of Fazlic's sons, were taken to Omarska. They have not returned. Muslim officials believe Omarska is a death camp.

In the detention center, Fazlic says he witnessed the execution of his next-door neighbors, Hadzic Ilijaz and his wife Ismeta. Ilijaz had been the local chairman of the Muslim SDA party, which had organized the town's resistance. "They demanded that he provide the names of all Muslim activists," Fazlic said. Ilijaz refused. Fazlic spoke matter-of-factly as he described what had happened to the Ilijaz family.

"They [the military] took electric drills and bored them into their chests," he said. The three children, ages 1, 3 and 5, were impaled on spikes. "We saw it with our own eyes," he said.

There were 200 men and women tied together, arm to arm, in a detention center in the village of Trnopolje near Kozarac. At night there were rapes. Guards entered with flashlights looking for young women, whom they took away for the night. "If anyone resisted, they were killed. Only a few did."

Serbian officials would not comment on the specifics of these allegations. Maj. Milovan Milutinovic, the army spokesman in Banja Luka, told *Newsday* last week, "In Kozarac there was a really big group of extremists. They were refusing any kind of negotiations about organizing community life. All attempts to find a peaceful solution failed. They openly resisted, so we answered them energetically."

Finally, the townspeople were deported on two sealed trains—one carrying 2,200 people and the other 1,600, according to Red Cross officials in the Bosnian town of Zenica where they eventually wound up before being brought to Zagreb. The deportees were segregated by sex except that children were allowed to stay with their mothers. The luckiest were the infants who were still nursing, Fazlic said. The unluckiest were the small children. "Most of the dead were children," he said. "They'd open the door, take the bodies out and dump them by the roadside. We weren't allowed to bury them."

His car was stiflingly hot. There was no water and little air. The men stripped off almost all their clothes. The train began as a convoy of five freight cars followed by a car of bearded men with machine guns who he believes belonged to the Serbian Chetniks, a militia force.

When the train reached Banja Luka a few hours down the line, the militia unit asked the army to take charge of the train, but its officers refused. Negotiations continued for three or four hours, and finally the militia opened the doors of a women's car. The army then provided an escort for the next leg of the journey, into the war zone. Then new guards took over the train.

"They opened the doors. They beat us, demanding money. They ripped earrings off the women. They grabbed anything they could." The refugees stayed an entire night and then proceeded to Maglaj on the same train.

Fazlic would like to return to Kozarac, what is left of it.

The Serbs have renamed it Radosavci. "It was one of the most beautiful cities in Bosnian Krajina," said an official of the Muslim SDA party in Banja Luka last week. "But now, if you Americans decide to intervene, we can present it to you as a golf course. It has been completely flattened."

❖

Death Camps

Survivors Tell of Captivity, Mass Slaughters in Bosnia

Zagreb, Croatia, August 2, 1992

The Serb conquerors of northern Bosnia have established two concentration camps in which more than a thousand civilians have been executed or starved and thousands more are being held until they die, according to two recently released prisoners interviewed by Newsday.

The testimony of the two survivors appeared to be the first eyewitness accounts of what international human rights agencies fear may be systematic slaughter conducted on a huge scale. *Newsday* has not been able to visit the camps. Neither has the International Red Cross or any other international agency.

In one concentration camp, a former iron-mining complex at Omarska in northwest Bosnia, more than a thousand Muslim and Croat civilians were held in metal cages without sanitation, adequate food, exercise or access to the outside world, according to a former prisoner who asked to be identified only as "Meho." The prisoners at the camp, he said, include the entire political and cultural elite of the city of Prijedor. Armed Serbian guards executed prisoners in groups of 10 to 15 every few days, he said.

"They would take them to a nearby lake. You'd hear a volley of rifles, and they'd never come back," Meho said.

"I think if these places are not death camps, we might have access to them," said Pierre Andre Conod, head of the International Committee of the Red Cross delegation in Zagreb, which oversees conditions in northern Bosnia.

"They'd have reason to show them to us if the conditions are acceptable." The Red Cross has gained access twice to what Bosnian Serbs have called a prisoner-of-war camp in Manjaca.

Yugoslavian Prime Minister Milan Panic sent word through a deputy that he could neither confirm nor deny the existence of death camps and favored the closing of all camps on all sides in the Bosnian war. The country Panic has taken over is a shadow of the former Yugoslavia and consists only of Serbia, which is accused of sponsoring the war in Bosnia, and tiny Montenegro.

Serbs, who claim the Bosnian region as their own, describe the policy of expelling Muslims and Roman Catholic Croats as "ethnic cleansing"; reports by the survivors interviewed by *Newsday* suggest this is a euphemism for a campaign of atrocity and brutal deportation at best.

In a second improvised camp, in a customs warehouse on the bank of the Sava River in the northeast Bosnian city of Brcko, 1,350 people were slaughtered between May 15 and mid-June, according to Alija Lujinovic, 53, a traffic engineer who was imprisoned at the camp. Guards at Brcko executed prisoners by slitting their throats or with firing squads, he said.

"Meho," 63, a building contractor from the nearby town of Kozarac, was coaxed out of hiding by a doctor from his hometown for a two-hour conversation with *Newsday* and Red Cross personnel on Friday. Meho said he was detained at Omarska for one week in June before being released, he thinks because of his age. He was held in an ore loader inside a cage roughly 700 square feet, along with 300 other men awaiting processing by their captors, he said. The metal superstructure contained cages stacked four high, separated by grates. There were no toilets, and the prisoners had to live in their own filth, which dripped through the grates.

Meho said three people tried to escape by jumping through an open pipe from the top cage to the ground, but all were shot after falling 60 feet to the ground. He said he also heard from other prisoners that during his week in the camp, 35 to 40 men had died in agony after being beaten.

International relief agencies said his statement, given to *Newsday* in the presence of officials of the Bosnian Red Cross-Red Crescent—was the first confirmation of their suspicions that Omarska is a death camp. They said they had heard rumors for more than a month about such camps, but no one had talked to a survivor.

The International Red Cross has been trying for more than two weeks to gain access to Omarska, Conod said, but Serb authorities in Bosnia have turned them down, saying they could not guarantee their safety. The Serb-controlled Bosnian army refused two weeks ago to take a *Newsday* reporter and a freelance photographer to Omarska.

The Red Cross has not yet applied to visit Brcko because, after withdrawing from Bosnia in May following the killing of a Red Cross official, its staff members returned to Banja Luka, the main city in northern Bosnia, and have not yet resumed full operations in eastern Bosnia.

Meho said that while he was at Omarska, from about June 3 to 10, prisoners filled each of the four cages in the ore loader, and other prisoners estimated the camp population at about 8,000. The official Bosnian State Commission on War Crimes, a government body set up to compile a record of war crimes, in a report last week to the UN High Commissioner for Refugees, estimated there were 11,000 prisoners at Omarska, making it the largest of the 94 camps known to the commission. It had no estimate of prisoners killed.

According to an eyewitness report quoted by the Bosnian Muslim charity Merhamet two weeks ago, thousands of men were also being held in an open outdoor pit that had been used for mining iron ore. Meho said other prisoners apparently were housed in an ore-separating building and in an administration center. He said he was not aware of prisoners being kept in the open, at least while he was there. Mirza Muftic, a geological engineer who helped design the mining facility, said the open pit would have been over a mile away, so Meho could not have seen it.

Last week, the UN High Commissioner for Refugees issued a report quoting a guard at Omarska as telling a UN monitor that the authorities planned to kill the prisoners at Omarska by exposing them to the elements.

"We won't waste our bullets on them. They have no roof. There is sun and rain, cold nights, and beatings two times a day. We give them no food and no water. They will starve like animals," the UNHCR said in an emergency report published Monday in Geneva in conjunction with a special conference on Bosnian refugees.

Like so many refugees, Meho said he was beaten regularly and witnessed atrocities while he was held at Omarska and at two other camps where he was detained briefly en route to Omarska. When interviewed here, he said he could hardly lift his left arm, and he flashed a nearly toothless grin, seven teeth having been knocked out during the beatings he described. Meho said the Bosnian Serb army had arrested him in his home town of Kozarac on May 27.

"They put Red Crosses on their sleeve and on the tanks and shouted, 'Give up. The Red Cross is waiting for you. You will be protected,'" he recalled. But as they went to buses, he said, soldiers stood at the entrance with truncheons. "There were three armed guards in each bus. They said if you raised your head, you'd get a bullet through it."

The camps had been hastily assembled. Meho was taken first to Keretem, a ceramics manufacturing plant in the town of Prijedor, and then to Ciglana, a brickworks next door, before being sent to Omarska. He said he was picked up because the authorities suspected he had two sons who had fought against the Serbs.

"The system was that they'd take you in for an interview and would say that you'll be set free if you tell about the others. Everybody was accusing the others to save themselves. But they didn't release anyone," he said.

In the ore loader at Omarska, people were crowded so tightly that "there was nowhere to lie down. You'd drowse off and fall against the next person." Bread was distributed every third day, a two-pound loaf for three people, and after a week prisoners were given a small cup of weak soup once a day.

In the close quarters, with no sanitation, all the men grew beards and all were infested by lice, he said. The prisoners were sorted by the different levels of the ore loader, and Meho's brother, a 51-year-old X-ray technician, was in the "B" level. Meho said he was in the "C" level. He said Friday that another recently released prisoner told him that his brother had died after Meho left.

He said guards took him out for questioning and beatings every other night. He said he knew the man who questioned him, a teacher from Bosanski Novi, and two other guards, one of them a waiter in a restaurant, but all pretended they did not know him. He said he never admitted that he had sons or a brother. When the interrogator asked him about his sons, he replied, "Comrade, I don't have any sons." The commander replied, "Don't call me comrade." Meho said he has two sons, one of whom remains in Bosnia.

Meho said all the soldiers grew long beards in the style of the Serbian Chetniks, a royalist military force during World War II. The commander himself did not threaten Meho's life, he said, but other soldiers did repeatedly. "They would say to us that for every Serb killed on the battlefield, we will take 300 of you."

He said he was the only person to get out of the "C" level, and it probably was due to his age. About 45 people from the "B" level were also removed, all of them men over 60, while able-bodied men between 18 and 60 were kept at the camp. He was taken to Trnopolje, a village between Omarska and Prijedor, which has been turned into a gigantic detention camp. Because of his condition when he arrived, Meho said other prisoners shunned him at first.

This squares with an account by the daughter of a prominent Prijedor city council member who witnessed a later arrival of people from Omarska. The woman, a professional who asked not to be named in order to protect relatives who remain behind, said in an interview before Meho's that a colleague had seen the released men and said, "They were all under 18 or over 60. For the first few days they had to be kept separate. They had lice, even on their eyebrows. They were completely exhausted and very thin."

The woman herself was in Trnopolje but was not jailed. She said the inmates at Omarska included professional women from Prijedor who apparently were being kept separately from the men in the administration building. Among them were dentists, gynecologists, "anyone of high standing." Now they are on a hunger strike, the professional says.

❖

Witness's Tale of Death and Torture

In Six-week Spree, at Least 3,000 Killed

Zagreb, Croatia, August 2, 1992

The Serb captors executed some of their Bosnian prisoners with pistols, but the preferred method was slitting throats, according to survivor Alija Lujinovic. Then the bodies would be stripped naked and thrown into the Sava River.

"They would say they are feeding the fish," he recalled.

The outcome was one of the worst recorded slaughters of the Serb-led war in Bosnia, according to the Bosnian State Commission on War Crimes. After a six-week killing spree, from the beginning of May to early June at the Brcko concentration camp and surrounding areas, at least 3,000 people were dead, the highest death toll at any of the 94 camps listed by the commission.

Lujinovic, a 53-year-old Muslim, said he was one of only 150 prisoners still alive of the 1,500 who had arrived at the beginning of May. After slaughtering nine-tenths of the prisoners, the guards turned on townspeople who had not been captured, he told *Newsday* during a two-hour interview Wednesday.

Then instead of tossing those bodies into the Sava, they had prisoners drive them to an animal feed plant, he said. Lujinovic said the prisoners didn't actually throw the corpses into the oven, but they had every reason to believe the bodies were being cremated for animal feed, for that day the air in Brcko would stink so badly you couldn't open the window.

Lujinovic was a traffic engineer employed by the city of Brcko in northeast Bosnia when the Yugoslav army, directed from Serbia, launched an assault to capture a land corridor through northern Bosnia in early May. He said he experienced nearly every form of humiliation the Serb captors inflicted on Muslim prisoners, from desecration of the local mosque to witnessing the murder and mutilation of male prisoners and the gang rape of Muslim women.

Sometimes the prisoners were subjected to horrible mutilations before they were tossed into the Sava. "The very worst day—and I saw it with my own eyes—was when I saw 10 young men laid out in a row. They had their throats slit, their noses cut off and their genitals plucked out. It was the worst thing I saw." A Serb guard appeared before the prisoners who were made to observe the killings; he had a homemade wire device with three prongs attached to a long handle. "He threatened to castrate us," Lujinovic said.

The first to be executed were the Muslim political party members and the Bosnian home guard, he said. "They called out names, took out the prisoners and started killing. We would hear three shots, and the man would not come back," Lujinovic recalled.

But they soon switched methods and began slitting throats of prisoners, he said. "They would tell them to lie down and put their head on a concrete block. The guards would cut their throats. I saw it with my own eyes." The bodies were positioned so that the blood flowed into the Sava. And finally, after about a month of executions, the guards started executing the townspeople, he said.

Lujinovic was saved, he said, because a benefactor, whom he would not identify, bought the release of 120 prisoners. In fact, he said, when the police chief came on June 23 and read out the names of the 120 prisoners to be released, his was not among them. But he knew the inspector of police, Dragisa Tesanovic, and he walked across the yard to him. "I asked him how he could keep me here. I said if I had been in his place and he in mine, I wouldn't keep him for even 24 hours. He said, 'You're right,' and got my papers."

Lujinovic said he escaped Bosnia by signing over all his property to the newly installed Serb authorities at a special office set up for the purpose. There he saw a Serb he knew named Zarko, who seemed astonished to see him.

"Good God. Are you still alive?" he recalled Zarko saying. After four hours of waiting, Lujinovic received a pass to leave Bosnia, and on July 13 he took the bus to northern Serbia and then left, via Hungary, for Croatia.

eportation train: Terrorized by Serb militia forces, the entire population
Kozluk, eastern Bosnia, fled to Serbia, where they were loaded onto an
3-car train chartered by the Serbian government for deportation to
ungary. Hungary blocked entry, and the train halted at Palic, northern
rbia, where mothers and infants disembarked for food. (Roy Gutman)

Manjaca, Bosnia-Herzegovina, July 1992: Newly arrested Muslim prisoners being shorn like sheep by the Serb guards at a "prisoner-of-war" camp in Serb-dominated north Bosnia. Of the estimated 3,000 prisoners, only a handful bore arms against the Serb conquerors, according to international relief workers. (Andree Kaiser/GAFF)

Manjaca: Hand-lettered sign on the barbed-wire perimeter fence warns of mines. (Andree Kaiser/GAFF)

Ethnic cleansing: Serb authorities deported thousands of Bosnians in sealed boxcars, robbed them en route, then ordered them to march through no-man's land into Muslim-held areas. Began Fazlic, 66, poses in a freight car in Zagreb similar to the one he traveled on for three days and nights. (Andree Kaiser/GAFF)

osanski Samac, Bosnia-Herzegovina: The screams and wails of prisoners eld in the Serb police station could be heard night after night across the ver in Slavonski Samac. Released prisoners there say they were beaten ightly by Serb guards, and some were ordered to eat their own feces. ndree Kaiser/GAFF)

Kalesija, eastern Bosnia: Bosnian government soldiers run for cover into mosque destroyed in Serb assault. (Andree Kaiser/GAFF)

Kalesija: Taking refuge from shelling in the mosque. (Andree Kaiser/GAFF)

Prijedor, northern Bosnia: Collecting firewood from the rubble of St. Joseph's Catholic Church, blown up during the overnight police curfew of August 29, 1992, minutes after a similar explosion destroyed the Prohaska Mosque nearby. (Boris Geilert/GAFF)

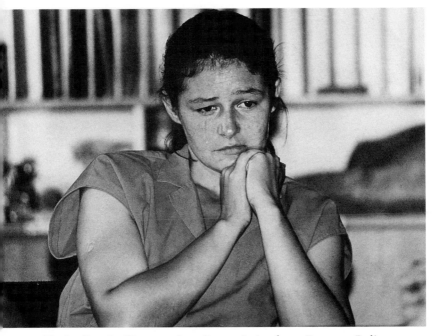

Tuzla, Bosnia-Herzegovina: Rape victim from Brezovo Polje, northern Bosnia. (Andree Kaiser/GAFF)

Tuzla: Muslim rape victims. (Andree Kaiser/GAFF)

Tuzla: A child asleep on the floor of the school gymnasium.
(Andree Kaiser/GAFF)

Tuzla: Mother and son at a refugee center. (Andree Kaiser/GAFF)

Tuzla: Their fathers and brothers were taken to concentration camps. Their mothers were sent alone across a minefield. Then the daughters were systematically raped and released. The Brezovo Polje rape victims, shown reunited with their mothers. (Andree Kaiser/GAFF)

Tuzla: Distraught, hurt, angry. Rape victims from Brezovo Polje.
(Andree Kaiser/GAFF)

Karlovac, Croatia: Two brothers, in the first group released from
Omarska, Kereterm and Trnopolje concentration camps in north
Bosnia, reunite with the daughter of one. (Andree Kaiser/GAFF)

Gulag

War against Muslim and Croat Civilians: Former Inmates of Serbian Forces Describe Atrocities

Slavonski Samac, Croatia, August 3, 1992

Night after night, the screams and wails of Muslim and Croat women and children detained by Serbians in Bosnia can be heard across the Sava. Trucks drive up near the river-front police station. There is screaming. The trucks drive off.

For men who were in the camps last spring, the cries are doubly haunting. From April to June, the sounds from across the river, they said, were of men screaming as they were beaten inside the police station.

Here on the Croatian side of the river, Muslim and Croat men who were released in prisoner exchanges have no idea what is happening to the women of Bosanski Samac. Are they being separated from their children? Are they being taken to other camps? Are they being prepared for exchanges?

Once these modest towns were linked by commerce, marriage and sports. But today the Sava has become a river of blood, as it was during World War II. The bridge lies in ruins, watched by Serbs from a guard post under the structure and by snipers armed with rocket-propelled grenades and high-powered rifles from positions atop the grain silos.

Daily, six or seven corpses float down the river between the twin towns, the men say, killed during the Serb advance into northern Bosnia. Four men who were prisoners across the river recall the sounds of spring—their own screams. They recall that the beatings intensified in the days before their release. Some of the tortures inflicted on them were unspeakable. After two hours of talks with four ex-prisoners, one handed a *Newsday* reporter a written statement describing how they had to watch the murder of 15 detainees and the torture of prisoners. On one occasion, the statement said, a prisoner was made to eat his own feces.

The camps were established as part of the Gulag set up by Serb forces who are now engaged in "cleansing" conquered territory of Muslims and Croats. These were not death camps as such, despite the reported blood orgy in which 15 men were executed. The four ex-prisoners estimated that 800 men were detained there, many dragged in from the streets while doing their morning shopping. They were brought to storage rooms in the police station, a farmers cooperative, the elementary school, the secondary school and the offices of the territorial defense.

An unusual aspect of the Samac camps was that as recently as last week their existence was unknown to the Bosnian government, which sent a list of 94 detention camps to the UN High Commissioner for Refugees. The omission suggests that the total number of camps in Bosnia may be a good deal higher than the number known to date.

The internment of civilians is flatly denied by the Serb leadership of Bosnia. "The Serbian side energetically denies the existence of camps for civilians anywhere in the Serbian Republic of Bosnia-Herzegovina," psychiatrist Radovan Karadzic, head of the Serb Democratic Party, said in a statement to *Newsday* on Saturday.

But a look at the prisoners, who emerged from detention that lasted two or more months with broken bones, impaired eyesight, organs damaged from the beatings, offered a graphic repudiation. H.D., 38, has a crease across his head where a guard struck him with an iron bar. He said guards may have singled him out for additional beatings because he had been a member of the Muslim political party SDA, but he said he was not interrogated even once during his 70 days of detention.

"We were beaten with iron bars, baseball bats, and truncheons, but we called the truncheons 'bananas,' for they represented a kind of relief." He would not give his name because his wife is being detained, as far as he knows, in the village across the river. One day a group of four Serb guards beckoned to him. They removed four baseball bats from a leather bag and began beating him. "I have watched baseball on TV, and they swung them as if they were hitting a ball, with both hands. That night I said good-bye to the world. I just wanted to die," he said.

One 61-year-old man asked to be identified only as "Survivor." His is a story of sadist depravity. "The victim was beaten over the head, neck, shoulders, back, chest, hips, feet, and arms—that is, over the entire body," he wrote. "Sometimes he was beaten by one man, sometimes by three, and sometimes even 10 policemen at the same time. They usually beat us during the daytime, sometimes in the room where we were housed and sometimes in the yard. . . ." After torture like this, the victim was covered with blood, and his back was blue and red from the blows.

Much of the treatment seems standardized in camps across northern Bosnia, judging from accounts by former prisoners. Detainees are packed into tiny storage rooms so tightly they could not lie down and at best could sleep only in shifts. Guards allowed them access to the toilet once a day if at all and fed them meager rations. But the pattern varied. In Bosanski Samac the guards would stand in a cluster and make the prisoner walk around them, each taking a swat at him with a two-by-four or a truncheon as he passed.

Personal Account of Terror

Slavonski Samac, Croatia, August 3, 1992

After a lengthy interview, a former prisoner at the Bosanski Samac detention camp handed *Newsday* a written statement describing torture he said he and other prisoners were subjected to by their Serbian jailers. Because of relatives still held in camps, the man insisted on being identified only as "Survivor."

"I was one of 800 prisoners held by the Serbian authorities of the so-called Serbian district of Bosanski Samac in their concentration camps. There were five of these jails or centers in Bosanski Samac.

"The prisoners were Croats, Muslims and Albanians, that is, people of non-Serb nationality. Among the prisoners there were women and old men, men of over 60 and one who was 73. Prisoners were not being brought from the battlefields as captives but from their homes. Practically all of them had to go through various kinds of torture: beatings, being kept in closed, hot, suffocating premises, denied drinking water and denied the use of the toilet, as well as poor nutrition.

"The beatings were at the beginning done by special forces, from Serbia. Later the job was taken over by policemen who guarded us. They were local Serbs who carried out their jobs far more brutally than the special units men. They beat us with iron bars, wooden two-by-fours and truncheons, iron and rubber devices devices for beating, with their feet, and they were wearing military boots, with their fists and hands.

"The victim was beaten over the head, neck, shoulders,

back, chest, hips, feet, and arms, that is, over the entire body. Sometimes he was beaten by one man, sometimes by three, and sometimes even 10 policemen at the same time. They usually beat us during the daytime, sometimes in the room where we were housed and sometimes in the yard. After torture like this, the victim was covered with blood, over the head and back, and his back was blue and red from the blows.

"Special forces would beat us during the day outside in the yard. Police guards usually beat us at night. They would take the victims out one by one, and three or four of them would throw themselves on him in the dark. And sometimes up to 10 policemen. They beat him with anything and everything, so that the victim's screams were horrible to listen to for us. Each of us feared we would be the next one they would beat.

"A victim who could still walk would be thrown back into the room like an animal, all bloodied and blue with bruises. There were times when the victims could not walk from the blows or had fallen unconscious, so two other prisoners would have to carry him into the room.

"I know that they beat one prisoner so long that at the end, one of the policeman hit him with a two-by-four over the forehead and he fell unconscious. This happened during the night, and two other prisoners brought him in in the morning. He only regained consciousness the following day around 10 in the morning.

"After we were let out of the jail through an exchange [for Serbian prisoners] and after medical checks, a large number of prisoners were found to have several broken ribs. The one who was hit with the two-by-four on the forehead had to have an operation on his head in Zagreb.

"Apart from beating us, they tortured us by preventing us from going to the toilet as the need arose; from having drinking water, and in other ways. The last month before the exchange we were getting only one meal a day, lunch.

Sometimes this lunch, the only meal in 24 hours, was a small slice of bread with jam.

"In their tortures they went so far as to make a prisoner eat sand. And they forced one prisoner to swallow his own feces, another to perform sex acts on a fellow prisoner.

"It was a terrible scene when one Special Force man from Serbia decided to show us, as he put it, how Chetniks slaughter their victims. While he selected his victim with a knife in his hands, every one of us thought he was going to be the victim. We stood there terrified while he made his choice. He selected as his victim one of two Albanian brothers, the younger of the two. He ordered him to crouch down on all fours and to spread out as far as he could in the middle of a circle that we were made to form around him. He tortured us and the victim horribly, psychologically by drawing his knife around on all sides of his neck but without cutting. Then he began to kick the victim with his feet and fists on the head and all other parts of his body.

"I think the most horrible night was the one between the seventh and eighth of May when a Serbian Special Force squad came to the farmers cooperative storerooms in Crkvini [three miles from Bosanski Samac and another of the five internment centers] and shot 15 of the 45 people there. When the door of the storeroom was forcibly opened, we were ordered, without the lights being turned on, to line up along one side of the room, which we did speedily.

"Another Special Force man shined a flashlight on us one by one, and the first Special Force man chose his victim, hitting him on the head with his gun and then shooting him and killing him. The people were collapsing on the floor in a heap, and blood was pouring across the concrete floor. When he finished his first round, he ordered the others who had survived to quickly line up on the other side of the room, which we did. He again began to choose and to shoot his victims. I know that in the second round he asked everybody their name and their occupation, and then he made his choice on those grounds, and then shot the people. About 15 people were left lying dead in that room. Around them on the concrete was a pool of their blood.

"Then they moved us over to the third side of this room, and they ordered the younger people to load the dead bodies on a truck, which had come up to the doorway. Then he told them to clean the blood off the floor, which they did. We spent that night in that same room.

"We kept the terrible story of what we saw there from the other prisoners, and we did not even talk about that horrible night among ourselves."

❖

Serbs' Death Camps

How the Guards Chose the Victims

Zagreb, Croatia, August 5, 1992

Serbian guards at the Omarska concentration camp in Bosnia daily executed dozens of Muslim and Croat prisoners from the thousands being held in at least three locations in the sprawling former mining complex, according to interviews conducted by *Newsday* yesterday.

Guards selected seven or eight victims at random each night using a flashlight in a darkened warehouse, where 600 to 700 were packed together, according to a 53-year-old Muslim camp survivor interviewed yesterday. The survivor, who asked to be identified only as "Hujca," said the only apparent trait the victims shared was their muscular build.

"The next morning they were not there," Hujca said. Guards returned the next day to select a team of young men to bury the dead, some of whom had been shot through the mouth, while others had their throats slit, he said. He did not witness the killings himself. On one occasion he saw eight corpses covered with blankets. On other days members of the burial crew told him what they had seen.

Hujca's narrative, along with a new indirect account obtained yesterday about prisoners kept in an outdoor pit at Omarska, added grisly new details to eyewitness accounts published by *Newsday* on August 2. *Newsday* described allegations of thousands of deaths at the Omarska camp and at a separate camp in Brcko in northeast Bosnia. The new disclosures added to an emerging picture of the Omarska camp and to what international human rights agencies fear may be slaughter on a huge scale. *Newsday* hasn't been able to visit the camps. Neither has the International Red Cross or any other international agency. The United Nations Security Council last night demanded that prison camps in the region be opened for impartial international inspection.

Serbian officials in Bosnia have denied that any civilians are being held in prison camps. Yugoslav Prime Minister Milan Panic, who presides over a government that consists only of Serbia and tiny Montenegro, acknowledges that prison camps are being maintained on all sides. He has said that he cannot confirm or deny the existence of death camps and favors closing all camps.

In an interview conducted yesterday, Hujca substantiated earlier allegations about the Omarska camp. He said he was held in a warehouse for 12 days in May, jammed into a room packed so tightly that no one could lie down to sleep. He had been a fighter with the Bosnian defense force but disposed of his submachine gun and was not detected when he joined townspeople from Kozarac, a town in northwest Bosnia conquered by Serb forces in May. But thousands of civilians were detained by Serbian units, and all of them ended up at Omarska.

When he arrived at the camp, Hujca said, he saw a prisoner who jumped through a plate-glass window in the camp administration building and landed on top of a soldier. "The guards near us shot a volley at him, but I think he got away." And shortly after arriving he saw guards club a man to death. He recognized the victim as the manager of the Kozarac sawmill.

Hujca was held in Omarska during the same period as another survivor named "Meho," whose testimony *Newsday* described on August 2. Both men said that 8,000 prisoners, most but not all of them men, were held at the time. The Bosnian government estimates that there are 11,000 prisoners there. Meho was held inside a metal cage that was part of an ore loader in the mine. Hujca was in a warehouse in another part of the facility.

Like the prisoners in the ore loader, those in the warehouse were malnourished, Hujca said. They received a tiny piece of bread every 24 hours.

In addition, an indirect account provided details of the conditions within a huge open pit where hundreds of prisoners were held. Prisoners were summoned by guards to climb more than 100 feet to the surface, never to come back, according to Fahrudin Ganic, 30, a member of the Bosnian Muslim defense force, quoting a 15-year-old Muslim boy who had been confined to the pit for over a week in mid-June. The boy did not know what became of them.

Ganic and two other Bosnian fighters who had recently arrived from north Bosnia also said they had witnessed a massacre in the village of Biscani just two weeks before in which at least 150 people were gunned down at short range by Serb forces.

The Muslim boy was from the village of Cerici, and Ganic was able to identify him only by his family name, Gredelje. He had been at Omarska for about a week and was released apparently because he was considered to be under age. Serb forces transferred him from Omarska to a nearby camp at Trnopolje and then released him to his home village, said Ganic. Two days after returning, the boy heard that he was about to be rearrested, and he escaped into the woods where he met the home guardsmen, Ganic said. Gredelje left Bosnia with a different group who headed south, according to Ganic.

This story of conditions in the pit supports two other indirect accounts cited earlier by *Newsday*. A resident of Banja Luka and a UN source said earlier that thousands were being held in the pit and were dying from starvation and exposure to the elements.

When it rains, the prisoners must stand in the red mud, for there is no shelter, Ganic said. There are no toilets, no beds, and the men must stand or crouch in close quarters with their bodily waste.

Stomach ailments are endemic, and the prisoners are fed like animals. The guards throw in about one loaf for roughly every eight prisoners. The only relief from the day's heat was that occasionally a guard would spray a hose at the detainees, Ganic said.

Ganic spoke to a *Newsday* reporter at the unofficial headquarters of the Bosnian defense forces in Zagreb along with two fellow guardsmen, who identified themselves only as "Mirsad," a 33-year-old attorney, and "Edwin," a 32-year-old carpenter. The three had recently escaped from north Bosnia after Serb forces broke through their defense lines.

❖

The State Department first said it had similar evidence of killings and torture in Serb detention camps and then retracted the statement, adding to the public furor over the disclosure. Finally, after a British television crew filmed emaciated prisoners in Omarska and other camps, President Bush publicly demanded that the authorities provide access to the camps for the International Red Cross. Inside Bosnia, Serb authorities closed down the Omarska camp and dispersed its prisoners to other camps. Under worldwide public pressure, the UN Security Council authorized member states to take military action to ensure the flow of food and medicine to Sarajevo and other Bosnian cities. The council also condemned "ethnic cleansing" as a violation of international law and the UN Human Rights Commission appointed Tadeusz Mazowiecki, a former Polish prime minister, to investigate allegations of massive human rights abuses. At a conference in London late that month, the Bosnian Serbs promised to close all detention camps for civilians, a pledge co-signed by the Bosnian Croats and the predominantly Muslim government.

Bosnia Rape Horror

Split, Croatia, August 9, 1992

Dressed in jungle fatigues and armed with knives and guns, the guards scoured the dark, crowded room with their flashlights, searching for girls to abduct for the night. Then one of them noticed 16-year-old S.T.

"Get up," he ordered, rifle in hand.

Her mother began to cry. But the guard knew how to put a stop to that. "—your mother," he said, drawing his knife.

S.T.'s mother fainted, and the teenager was led at gunpoint with three other girls to a covered green truck, where she was raped three times.

The triple rape of the Muslim teenager in June was only one among thousands, maybe tens of thousands, of assaults that officials of Bosnia-Herzegovina fear have been carried out against Muslim and Croat women in the Serb prison camps of northern Bosnia.

Reports of rape have been so extensive that some analysts think it was systematic. Sevko Omerbasic, leader of the Muslim community in Croatia and Slovenia, who is in direct touch with hundreds of refugees every week, has reached that conclusion. "There is more and more evidence that all the young woman have been raped," he told *Newsday* in a recent interview.

There are an astonishing number of reports of gang rapes of girls just above the age of puberty. And unlike S.T., who was released from the Trnopolje camp in late June, thousands, perhaps tens of thousands, of rape victims may remain in these prisons set up in schools, factories and villages.

The Bosnian government estimated Friday that 200,000 people, mostly women, children and the elderly, are being held. Officials said they know of at least one or more camps reserved entirely for women and children, but they said there is no way to estimate how many have been raped.

Radovan Karadzic, head of the Serb Bosnian government, denied that there are any detention camps for civilians in Bosnia and added that no women or children were detained at any location. Asked about the reports of systematic rape, he told *Newsday*: "There are six places in Sarajevo alone where they [the Muslims] are raping Serb women. We Serbs know what is going on."

For her family, S.T.'s ordeal was another wrenching trauma in the tragedy that has befallen them since Serbs began the "ethnic cleansing" of northern Bosnia. The family has been virtually destroyed, and no one knows if it can be put back together. Serbs took S.T.'s father, a house painter, to the Omarska camp, where witnesses have reported killings of large numbers of prisoners. No one knows where her 21-year-old brother is or if he is alive.

The conquering force took over their house in Kozarusa and almost certainly ransacked it. The fate of the 14 relatives who remained behind in the northwest Bosnian region is uncertain at best. And S.T. must forever live with the trauma of that night in June at the Trnopolje camp.

Yet despite all they have been through, or perhaps because of it, the mother and daughter agreed to the suggestion of a doctor to talk to a *Newsday* reporter on Thursday. Their only condition was that they be identified only by initials.

The evening at the modest apartment of S.T.'s uncle in this Adriatic seaport might have proved cathartic had it not been for the videotape unexpectedly shown on television giving a first look at the inmates at the Omarska and Trnopolje prison camps. As she watched the emaciated prisoners barely able to lift their soup spoons with the colored liquid that had been sloshed into their bowls, M.T., the 42-

year-old mother, started weeping, and S.T. sat quietly, occasionally sobbing.

The tape was run a second time, and they searched the faces of the prisoners behind the barbed-wire fences for the missing father and brother. Neither appeared. S.T. looked crestfallen. No one said a word.

The rape was also a fairly speechless affair. The three guards were clean-shaven, S.T. said. Each had a "four S's" tattoo on his hand, initials of the slogan under which the Serb military has committed mayhem in Bosnia: "Only solidarity saves the Serbs." The three soldiers and the four girls climbed into the back of the military truck, which came with a driver, and they stopped outside a gas station a few miles from the camp. S.T. was crying, and the guards left her on the truck. The other three girls, who were older, were led into a house that had once belonged to a prominent Muslim in the town and now served as the brothel for the camp guards. There were about a dozen other men inside.

The soldier remaining behind ordered S.T. to disrobe and lie down on the floor of the truck. He left his clothes on and forced her to have intercourse. When the first soldier was satisfied, he fetched his friend. Finally, the third one took his turn.

"What are you doing?" S.T. recalled asking the last of the rapists.

"That's what your people are doing to us as well," he said in reply. He thought a minute and said, "I'll get you out of here." He told her to get dressed. Before driving off he called out to his buddies, "I'm going to get some more." Then he drove her back to the crowded room in the school at the Trnopolje camp and left her there. He searched the room with his flashlight, and the process began all over again. It was the second of three visitations that night.

In a way S.T. was lucky. The other girls remained inside the brothel, and one of them told S.T. she had been raped by 12 different men that night. The soldiers brought them back at about 3:30 A.M.

S.T. and her mother left Trnopolje camp a few days later, loaded like cattle into closed boxcars for a day-long trip through a war zone into Muslim-held territory. After walking, driving, being bused and undergoing an eight-hour train journey to Zagreb, they arrived at the city's main railway station destitute, hungry and weak. S.T. fainted on the platform and was taken to a gynecological hospital. When she appeared at a suburban clinic in Zagreb on June 25, she was in shock. "She stood like a stone," the doctor, Vanda Panjkota, recalled. The doctor prescribed a hormonal anti-pregnancy drug. She didn't ask any questions. "It was non-verbal communication. I don't think she said more than two or three words," Panjkota said.

S.T.'s mother was also along and could hardly speak.

"She was speaking in sign language," the doctor recalled, "as if to say, 'Please help us.'

"Two other nurses observed the scene. We looked at her and wanted to cry with her," said the doctor.

The Rapes of Bosnia

"We Want the World to Know"

Tuzla, Bosnia-Herzegovina, August 23, 1992

Serb forces in northern Bosnia systematically raped 40 young Muslim women of a town they captured early this summer, telling some of their victims they were under orders to do so, the young women say. Statements by victims of the assault, describing their ordeal in chilling detail, bear out reports that the Serb conquerers of Bosnia have raped Muslim women, not as a by-product of the war but as a principal tactic of the war.

"'We have orders to rape the girls,'" Mirsada, 23, one of 20 young victims interviewed by *Newsday,* said the young man who abducted her told her. He said he was "ashamed to be a Serb" and added that "everything that is going on is a war crime," she said.

Hafiza, also 23, said she sought to dissuade the soldier who raped her. "I tried crying and begging," she said. "I said, 'You have a mother and a sister, a female in the family.' He said nothing. He didn't want to talk. Then he said, 'I must. I must.' I said, 'You must not if you don't want to.'" But she was unable to stop him.

The incident involved 40 young women from Brezovo Polje, a small town on the Sava River where conquering forces marched in, seized all the civilians and dispatched them according to age and gender to their assigned fate.

The rape victims were interviewed in a refugee center, their only haven after the destruction of their homes, their families and the basis of their economic survival. They agreed to be quoted and photographed provided they were identified only by first name and age.

"We want the world to know about our truth. All mothers. All women," said Senada, 17, who wrote a statement by hand and gave it to the chief gynecologist at Tuzla Hospital with the request that she pass it on to *Newsday*. "I wouldn't want anyone else to have the same experience. It is worse than any other punishment in the world."

The Brezovo Polje episode is only one of a number of indications of a pattern of systematized rape during the Serb conquest of Bosnia. In separate interviews in Tuzla, four young women from the village of Liplje, near Zvornik, said their Serb captors had detained them in a makeshift bordello where three or more men raped them every night for 10 nights. A leading Bosnian women's group has charged that upward of 10,000 Bosnian women are currently being held in Serb detention camps where their captors rape them repeatedly, although that has not been independently confirmed. Another pattern is the rape of pregnant women and some middle-aged women.

Dr. Melika Kreitmayer, leader of the gynecological team that examined 25 of the 40 victims from Brezovo Polje, said she and her colleagues are convinced that the object of the rapes was "to humiliate Muslim women, to insult them, to destroy their persons and to cause shock. . . . These women were raped not because it was the male instinct. They were raped because it was the goal of the war," she said. "My impression is that someone had an order to rape the girls." She cited as proof that some young women said they had been taken to a house and not raped but were instructed to tell others that they had been raped.

Kreitmayer, who is of Muslim origin and whose team includes a Serb and a Slovene doctor, made those assertions without any sign of objection from her colleagues. "We are shocked by what we have heard," commented her Serb colleague, Dr. Nenad Trifkovic.

According to the young women, the rapists discussed the assaults with their victims as a mission they had to accomplish. Many of the men fortified their resolve by taking white pills that appeared to stimulate them, the women said. The men's claim that they were operating under orders was reinforced when a new group of irregular forces arrived that owed its allegiance to one of the most savage of the warlords, Vojislav Seselj, a militant nationalist from Sarajevo. The leaders of the original group tried to protect the women of Brezovo Polje from the Seselj followers, the women indicated.

"'Don't worry. The girls have been raped once,'" Zlata, 23, recalled one of the officers telling the Seselj followers.

According to the victims, preparations for the mass rape began early on the morning of June 17 when Serb soldiers in army uniforms and masks piled out of their minivans and rounded up the Muslims of Brezovo Polje for ethnic cleansing. They loaded the able-bodied men from 18 to 60 onto buses and sent them for interrogation to Luka, a notorious Serb-run detention camp in nearby Brcko where nine in 10 prisoners were slaughtered, according to a survivor interviewed by *Newsday*.

Then they packed about 1,000 women, children and old people into eight buses, drove them around the countryside for two days and held them under armed guard for four terrifying nights without food or water in a parking lot in the nearby town of Ban Brdo, the victims said. Serb soldiers returning from the front invaded the buses every night and led off women and girls to an unknown location at knifepoint, recalled Senada, 17. "They threw them out in the morning, and their clothes were torn, and they were covered with blood," she said.

Finally the group arrived in Caparde, where about 50 Serb irregulars, bearded followers of a warlord named Zeljko Arkan, robbed the mothers and forcibly separated them from their daughters. The mothers were taken by bus and deposited in a war zone. Meanwhile, in the Osnovo furniture warehouse in Caparde, where the daughters were held, the men, mostly with long beards in the style of the World War II Serbian royalist force known as the Chetniks, selected what one of the rapists said were the 40 prettiest young women of Brezovo Polje and raped them in groups of 10.

Hejira, 21, said she asked Dragan, the man who raped her, why they were doing it. "He said we were the cleanest convoy that passed Caparde, the prettiest and most attractive, and that they couldn't let us pass because we were so beautiful." The victims were ages 15 to 30, with wholesome looks, careful dress and gentle manners.

"They would come by and tap us on the shoulder," recalled Hejira. "They told everyone else that we had gone to 'fetch water.' Some of the girls came back two hours later. Some the next morning. And each of them sat down and cried," she said.

The mothers arrived in Tuzla on June 23, distraught about their missing daughters and traumatized by the journey, which began with another bus ride and ended with a forced 12-mile walk through a war zone on a road littered with human corpses and animal carcasses. Their daughters arrived four days later, after a forced walk across a mined road with several elderly people, a number of whom died en route, they said.

The young women were exhausted and in a state of shock, doctors said. Most, according to the gynecological team that later examined them, had vaginal infections of staphyllococcus and other bacteria that originate in dirt or fecal matter. Almost every one of the 20 women interviewed by *Newsday* reported that the men who raped them were filthy and smelly, and in some cases had blood on their bodies.

The health and psychological stresses on the young women of Brezovo Polje are only part of their tragedy, for each is missing a father or a brother as well as the material basis of their lives. They are women in the prime of life, but few have anywhere to go; and the rapes have shaken their confidence. Almost every one broke into tears as she talked over several days to this reporter.

Their trauma is not over, for as Kreitmayer noted, many of them may become pregnant. The hospital will provide hormonal drugs to induce abortion, she added.

The deepest hurt seems to be moral shame. These women were from the countryside where premarital sex is prohibited, and Kreitmayer confirmed that all but one had been virgins at the time they were raped. Most of them think they have been ruined for life.

"We all feel that we lost everything," said Heira, 25. "We have been abandoned. We have been imperiled. Every woman, if she is raped, has to feel the same."

Satka, 20, said she despised the man who raped her "because he had no feeling for me. I wasn't his girlfriend. It was savagery." She said she felt shame because "I was an honest girl. I was a virgin. I gave it to someone who didn't deserve it. Someone whom I love deserves it. But not a savage."

Meira, 17, said the man who raped her threatened her with a hand grenade. "Mine put a grenade in my hand. He told me, 'All Serbs are good, and I am a good Serb.' And if I didn't agree, he could kill both of us with a bomb." The young man took the grenade back and put it on the table. Meira said she assumed he was ordered to rape her. He did not apologize "but said that he had to do it. He said it was better for me that he did it than the followers of Seselj, who would rape 10 men to one woman."

No such excuse seemed to be forthcoming in the rape of several pregnant women, who were so shattered that they asked to have their babies aborted.

Kreitmayer said one nurse from Brezovo Polje had lost her mother, father, husband, and 4-year-old child "in front of her eyes." The woman told doctors the Serb conquerors decided not to kill her but brought her to their military hospital. "She worked every day for them, but every night she was raped. She was sick. She was desperate. She told them she was between two and three months pregnant. But it meant nothing to them," Kreitmayer said. The woman came to the gynecological clinic "so sick that she desperately wanted an abortion," the doctor said.

For the young women of Brezovo Polje, shame alternates with anger. Each time this reporter returned to the school where they are living, a larger group of victims decided to join in the discussion. Rape had been so rare over the years in Bosnia that there are few professional counselors, and Kreitmeyer said this was the first appearance of mass rape and aggression toward women.

The victims say that right now they would like to be anywhere but in Bosnia-Herzegovina. Most say that once they leave here, they do not plan to return ever again.

Victims Recount Nights of Terror at Makeshift Bordello

Tuzla, Bosnia-Herzegovina, August 23, 1992

For five nights, Almira Ajanovic says, she was raped by Serb soldiers inside the temporary bordello they had set up in her home village of Liplje, three men every night.

"They took a knife and cut my dress open," the 18-year-old woman said, recalling how it began. The men, paramilitary troops with long beards in the style of Chetniks, the World War II Serb royalists, had stripped to the buff, and two pinned her to the bed as the third raped her. Then they switched places, each watching the others perform.

It continued for five nights, with different men each time, until the sixth, when they heightened the humiliation by raping Almira in front of her father. "That Chetnik said that he was going to marry me. My father kept silent," she recalled. Afterward the soldiers took her father to the toilet of the house and hung him by his neck, legs and hands until a neighbor rescued him 24 hours later.

Almira said she was unable to look him in the face after the incident. "I didn't want to see my father again for one month," she said. "I still cannot talk about this with him."

Liplje, a mainly Muslim village near the city of Zvornik, had fewer than 500 inhabitants. According to Dr. Melika Kreitmayer, chief of the rape study group at the Tuzla Hospital Gynecological Institute, practically every woman in the village was raped. The incidents occurred at the end of May while more than 400 of the villagers were held in a large house that Serb forces expropriated from a prominent local Muslim. Most of the rapists were Serb neighbors, but a few were from Serbia, the victims said.

A 57-year-old mother of six appeared at the institute and reported she had been raped twice nightly for 10 days. "She was very desperate when she came in, under psychological pressure so heavy that she couldn't live with it," Kreitmayer said. "She fears she has infections. She has an unconscious fear of being pregnant."

The woman, who would not give her name, sobbed as she described what had happened to her. "Eight of them came," she said. "I was alone. I was trying to open the rooms to show them there was no one in the house, and then one of them said, 'Undress yourself.' He attacked me from behind."

Both local police officials and the gynecological institute doctors said they are convinced the accounts of rapes in Liplje are true, based on medical examinations, questioning of victims and cross-checking. Almira and three friends were so angered by what happened to them that they agreed to be identified by full names and ages.

One of their best friends, Nezira Fahric, 17, was raped and then strangled to death, they said. Her mother, Hanifa Fahric, 50, wrote a statement and gave it to Kreitmayer to be made available to this reporter. "My daughter was strangled. We found her on the couch with her arms at her neck. They raped her and strangled her. It was probably our neighbors who did it," she said. "She was very beautiful. She had finished primary school."

Ziba Hasanovic, 18, said she was taken to the makeshift bordello on the second night of the Serb occupation. "That night I was raped by one man, who took my virginity, and then by three others," she said. "From the third night we were treated as if we were slaves. Our mothers were suddenly 'mothers-in-law.'"

Ziba said she spent her days in the bordello kitchen, baking bread. "Only two nights I was not raped," she said. She said the men who raped her were "dirty and on drugs," and she knew them by name. "I knew all of them who did it. They were my neighbors," she said.

Jasmina Feric, 20, witnessed the murder of her grandfather. "They cut off his ears, then his throat. They threw him behind the house," she said. She was allowed to live at her parents' house but was taken away each night to the bordello.

Sevlata Ajanovic, 18, was also employed as a cook. "I was raped every night," she said. She asked one captor why they suddenly turned on them. "The answer was that he had to do it. He said, 'Because you are Muslims, and there are too many of you.'"

Like other rape victims, the young women of Liplje believe their lives as future mothers and wives are over. "Everyone who is with us now [other refugees] does not believe we were forced," Sevlata said. "And they think we are going to go with them [the Serbs] again. We can't imagine marriage as a normal thing. We know that the man will always be suspicious."

Almira said one of her captors told her they wanted to "plant the seed of Serbs in Bosnia." Today she describes her feelings only as anger and shame.

"I am very ashamed," Jasmina said. "We will be afraid of making love again our whole lives."

Ziba, alone of the four, was in a state of fury. "I am angry. I want revenge," she said.

❖

Unholy War

Serbs Target Culture and Heritage
of Bosnia's Muslims

Tuzla, Bosnia-Herzegovina, September 2, 1992

Shortly after the Serbian army swept into eastern Bosnia last April, a bearded soldier climbed the minaret of the Rijecanska mosque in the town of Zvornik, hung a skull-and-crossbones flag out the window and placed a cassette on the recorder. From the tower where the Muslim call to prayer formerly sounded five times a day, bloodcurdling Serbian nationalist songs blared forth: "If you're not with us, we will kill you. We will slit your throats" and "You're a liar if you say Serbia is small."

"I wanted to destroy the minaret," said Asic Akim, a police commander from Zvornik who witnessed the scene for the 20 days and nights that he and colleagues held a Muslim position on a nearby hill. "But my colleagues stopped me." Numerous refugees from Zvornik contacted by *Newsday* corroborated his story.

The Serb-led war against Bosnia began in Zvornik and other towns along the Drina River. And almost from the very first, it was accompanied by an assault against the Muslim religious and cultural tradition, an assault whose impact has become clear as scholars examine the pattern of destruction. Muslim clergymen have been dispersed, imprisoned or killed, according to a variety of Muslim sources. National libraries and religious seminaries have been destroyed. And Bosnian scholars estimate that well over half of the mosques, historical monuments and libraries that comprise a six-century-old religious and cultural heritage have been wiped out.

No international agency has been able to study the extent of the damage, according to Ron Redmond, spokesman for the UN High Commissioner for Refugees. He visited Sanski Most in northeast Bosnia and noticed a mosque that had been completely dynamited. "Someone had gone to quite some length to reduce it to a pile of stone. But I can't say how widespread the practice was."

Numerous accounts compiled from Muslim expellees indicate that before they were destroyed, many houses of worship were desecrated.

In Novo Selo, a village near Zvornik, Serb troops rounded up 150 women, children and old people, and forced them at gunpoint into the local mosque. In front of the captives they challenged the local community leader, Imam Memic Suljo, to desecrate the mosque, Akim said, quoting eyewitness accounts. They told him to make the sign of the cross, eat pork and finally to have sexual intercourse with a teenage girl. Asic said that Suljo refused all these demands and was beaten and cut with knives. His fate is unknown.

In Bratunac, about 30 miles south, Imam Mustafa Mojkanovic was tortured before thousands of Muslim women, children and old people at the town's soccer stadium, according to a sworn account by witnesses quoted by the imam of Tuzla, Efardi Espahic. Serb guards also ordered the cleric to cross himself, Espahic said. When he refused, "they beat him. They stuffed his mouth with sawdust, poured beer in his mouth and then slit his throat," Espahic told *Newsday*.

Bosnian Serb leader Radovan Karadzic did not respond to repeated requests for comment.

The assault against Bosnia's Islamic heritage has been a largely unreported facet of the "ethnic cleansing" campaign, for it occurred in areas now occupied by the Serb conquerers. But accounts by refugees and data collected by the

Bosnian government, Bosnian scholars and Muslim leaders point to an irreplaceable loss. An official list of 115 destroyed and damaged mosques and other cultural objects, obtained by *Newsday* from *Behar,* a new Bosnian cultural affairs monthly, covers only the first six weeks of the war.

"It is terrible. It is unbelievable from the point of view of the history of art and architecture," commented Bogdan Bogdanovic, a Serbian architect and ex-mayor of Belgrade. "Beautiful cities have been completely destroyed and an enormous number of historic buildings. It is a great crime against civilization, a disgrace for my people and for the army which does that."

The destroyed or damaged treasures include the oldest, the most famous and the most beautiful mosques in Bosnia, according to the official Bosnian list and numerous other sources. All 14 mosques in and around Foca, among them the Aladza (the colored mosque), built in 1550 and said to be one of the most beautiful mosques in Europe, were destroyed, as was the Ustikolina mosque near Foca, built in 1448, the oldest mosque in Bosnia; 13 mosques in Mostar, all built between 1528 and 1631—among them the Karadjoz-Begova mosque, built in 1557.

Priceless treasures in Sarajevo have been damaged or destroyed: the Gazi Husref Beg mosque, built in 1530, the Imperial mosque, founded in 1450 and rebuilt in 1565, the Ali Pasha mosque from the same period, and a dozen smaller mosques of similar age. Serb artillery badly damaged the Gazi Husref Beg library, from about 1530, and the century-old city hall, which contained the national library. They completely destroyed the library of the Oriental Institute and the new Islamic seminary and also assaulted nearly every library at Sarajevo University.

Some of the Gazi Husref Beg library collection was saved, but elsewhere, most of the collections, including rare books and manuscripts in the Oriental Institute, were destroyed, according to Smail Balic, a leading scholar of Bosnian art history and a retired curator in the Austrian State Library in Vienna.

The pattern is repeated across Bosnia. According to figures cited by the head of the Islamic community in Zagreb, 200 mosques were destroyed and another 300 damaged between April and late July. The Bosnian Institute in Zurich, an independent scholarly institution, estimates that in areas of Serb occupation, 90 percent of the mosques have been destroyed.

Sevko Omerbasic, the mufti, or Muslim community leader, of Zagreb, said that statistics compiled by Islamic officials through the end of July indicate the Serb occupiers executed 37 imams, sent 35 to concentration camps and expelled 300 from Bosnia.

Bosnia has had a unique religious identity for nearly a millennium. Its state church from the twelfth to the fifteenth centuries was Bogomilism, a heretic Christian sect that rejected the Roman Catholic hierarchy and liturgy and preached pacifism and puritanism. Bosnian scholars say the Bogomils may have been the original Protestants, helping to inspire reformers in Bohemia and France. But the Bogomils were under constant pressure from the Roman Catholic and Orthodox churches, and Turkey appeared as a rescuer just as Catholic Hungary launched a Crusade in the fifteenth century. During the Turkish conquest, the Bogomils sought sanctuary in Islam, and the Turks allowed local practices to be absorbed into what became a unique Bosnian form of Islam.

Under both Turkish and Austrian rule, Bosnia was a sanctuary of tolerance in the Balkans, where Muslims, Roman Catholics and Orthodox Christians lived side by side. Jews fleeing the Spanish Inquisition settled in Bosnia and in 1966 celebrated their four-hundredth anniversary as a community in Sarajevo.

Kristallnacht for the Bosnian Muslims came not in one or two nights, as it did for Germany's Jews in November 1938, but was spread over many months, according to information now available. In Zvornik, where it all started on April 8, Serb forces destroyed or damaged 19 mosques in and around the city and at least 50 in other towns and cities nearby, according to information compiled in Tuzla, the biggest Muslim-ruled territory in Bosnia. The destruction continues. The Rijecanska mosque in Zvornik was blown up in late August, according to Izet Nakicevic, head of the "Zvornik Club," which gathers expellees from that city, in Zagreb.

The Serb forces, with overwhelming firepower, apparently targeted mosques for reasons that had nothing to do with military strategy. A great many mosques, including some of the best known, were blown up after Serbs occupied the towns, numerous Bosnian sources said.

According to expellees' reports cited by the mufti of Belgrade, Effendija Hadzi Hamdija Jusuf Pahic, the Aladja mosque was damaged by mortars during the Serb assault in mid-April but survived because of its stone construction. Early in July the Serbs planted dynamite around the site and blew it up. Then they bulldozed the rubble, he said. Today, grass is growing on the site. The Serbs also blew up Ustikolina with dynamite at the end of June and damaged the Ferhadija in Banja Luka in May.

"Our clear impression is that they are not destroying some historical monuments but every historical monument that represents the culture, tradition and continuity of a people," said Zehrid Ropic, a Tuzla architect who is compiling a list of destroyed monuments in northeast Bosnia.

Balic concurred. "They want to eliminate all traces of the past—of the Bosnian tradition, the Turkish tradition, and the Austrian tradition," he said.

According to accounts of Muslim expellees, mosques were used by the Serbs as prisons, slaughterhouses and morgues. Alija Lujinovic, 53, who was one of the witnesses quoted in an August 2 *Newsday* report on concentration camps in Bosnia, said that before he was taken to Brcko

Luka, he was held for four days, along with 150 to 180 men, in a mosque in Brcko. "They didn't let us go to the toilet. We had to relieve ourselves in the mosque, in the sacred ablution basin," he said. "They gave us no food for 48 hours and then served us pork." Then, he said, "they beat the prisoners there."

According to Espahic, who visited Kozluk subsequently, Serbs have since moved into the homes that had been occupied by Muslims. In the village of Kozluk, near Zvornik, Serbs set up a grill to serve roast pork in the forecourt of the mosque, according to Imam Espahic of Tuzla. *Newsday* reported on July 2 that all inhabitants of Kozluk had been taken to Serbia and loaded in a sealed train to be deported to Hungary.

The suddenness of the Serb onslaught caught Muslims in Bosnia unarmed and unprepared, and its ferocity has left them reeling. The religious leadership is embittered that the West has stood by without offering any help, instead imposing an arms embargo indiscriminately against all parties in the fighting.

"It is the shame of civilization to permit this, in a country that has been internationally recognized," said Espahic. He said President George Bush will intervene only if it will help his election campaign. "It is the hypocrisy of the West to recognize this sovereign republic and not want to protect it, not help us with arms so we can help ourselves. We don't want any help if we can get arms. We have a right to self-defense."

Omerbasic, the mufti of Zagreb, believes that the West is uninterested in Bosnia because it does not care about the fate of the only sizable Muslim community in Europe.

Acting Secretary of State Lawrence Eagleburger, during a news conference in London last week, did not address the issue directly but acknowledged that there is no question the Muslim world is upset about what is happening to Muslims in Bosnia. "There are limits to what we, or the West, are able to do at this stage," he said.

Richard Holbrooke, an assistant secretary of state in the Carter administration and now an adviser to Democratic presidential candidate Bill Clinton, recently visited northern Bosnia. "If the situation were reversed, and Christians or Jews were being attacked in Bosnia, there would be a lot more concern," Holbrooke said.

❖

The assault on sacred buildings continued well into 1993. In Zvornik, where the principal mosque once stood, there is now a clearing. Serbs blew up the Prohaska mosque in Prijedor, the Ferhadiya in Banja Luka, the mosques in Bijelina, and most other locations they occupied. The London Guardian *estimated in mid-June that 800 mosques had been destroyed. In most instances the sites have been leveled and the rubble removed.*

Back from the Dead

Freed Prisoners Detail Massacres

Karlovac, Croatia, October 4, 1992

After four traumatic months in captivity, the first large group of survivors of Serb-run concentration camps in Bosnia has reached freedom with eyewitness accounts that confirm charges of mass murders of civilians during the Serb conquest.

Jasmin Kaltak, 22, said he had volunteered for a work detail from the Kereterm concentration camp in late July to "harvest the wheat." What he harvested, he said, were bodies. Kaltak said that during three days he and another prisoner buried children as young as 2 years old and loaded 250 to 300 corpses of men and women into trucks from homes in seven Muslim villages south of Prijedor. Kaltak said there were 14 other two-man teams doing such work, which suggested that thousands of people may have been executed during the ethnic cleansing of the villages.

Mirsad Sinanbegovic, 35, recounted the night of July 22 when he said Serb guards fired gas bombs into a large room in a factory building in which he was held at Kereterm, then machine-gunned everyone who came to the front gasping for air. Sinanbegovic said that about 125 people were killed and 45 wounded in the massacre, but that the wounded were loaded into trucks along with the dead and never seen again. Some of the victims were as young as 13, he said. "There was so much blood, we had to take our shoes off," he said.

Sinanbegovic said he was one of 90 survivors and that he had saved himself by hitting the floor when the gas came in, as he had been taught to do in the army. Bodies fell on top of him, he said.

"I can't describe the shrieking," said Kaltak, who was in the room next door. "Some of the wounded people begged to be killed." The 1,561 former detainees, most of them Muslims, were brought to this western Croatian town from the detention camp at Trnopolje late Thursday and early Friday under the auspices of the International Red Cross. In a random sampling of about a dozen former prisoners, each one said he had been beaten or tortured or witnessed a killing. They had been arrested unarmed at home or at a friend's house and while in detention had never been charged with any crime.

The men gave interviews from within a crude wooden pen that Croatian authorities had erected on the main square in this city 40 miles southwest of Zagreb to supervise them until international relief agencies can resettle them abroad.

Esef Dzenanovic stood sobbing as ex-detainees all around him tearfully hugged and kissed arriving friends and relatives. No one had shown up to see the 33-year-old welder, and he took that as proof that Serb forces had raped his wife, his mother and his sister, and then killed them along with his two sons, ages 6 and 9. Dzenanovic had already heard separate accounts of the slaughter of his family from a Muslim neighbor and a Serb friend. "What am I to do now? What do you suggest?" he asked.

Also among the former detainees were six survivors of a widely reported massacre at Skender Vakuf on August 21. More than 200 Trnopolje camp inmates were shot and dumped in a ravine near the north Bosnian town of Skender Vakuf while being escorted by Serb security forces to Muslim-held Travnik, witnesses said.

M.M., a man who would identify himself only by his initials, said he was ordered with others to kneel at the edge of the ravine. "They started shouting insults and shooting," he said. "I jumped into the ravine. Luckily, I fell in an area that wasn't so steep. I rolled down, pretending to be dead. I found a corpse and dragged the man's body over me."

He said he started edging down the ravine toward a small stream. When the guards saw him moving, they began shooting, he said, but the body protected him. "I could feel the bullets hitting his body," he said. "I lay there two hours, pretending to be dead. I didn't dare move. They continued shooting." After three days of wandering in the nearby forests, M.M. was arrested by local police. They questioned him and then took him to the hospital at Skender Vakuf, where he was treated for his wounds but also beaten by local and military police.

Kaltak said he and nine others of the 250 men in his room had volunteered for the "wheat harvest" detail. The guards then seized another 20 at random to complete the work detail. They drove to the village of Tukovi, where they collected firewood "for the wives of Serb soldiers at the front," and then to Sredeci, where they began the grisly three-day task of collecting corpses, he said. "The bodies were in front of the houses and inside, and many were behind the houses," he recalled. The prisoners buried children as young as 2 years old behind the houses but loaded the corpses of the women and men "that were fresh and had not been infested by maggots" into trucks. Kaltak said he did not know where the corpses were taken.

Then they went to other villages. "The most corpses were in Biscani, Zecovi and Carakovo," he said. Most of the victims were men, he said. Their hands were tied with wire behind their backs. Corpses that had begun to decompose or had maggots were collected by prisoners and placed three to five in a pile, he recalled. A chemical officer in an army uniform and protective headgear would spray the pile with a white liquid, then light the pyre. The corpses would burn down to soot.

The police chief of Prijedor, Simo Drljaca, asked last

month to comment on estimates that up to 30,000 people were killed in his region, said he had no figures at all for the number of dead.

Kaltak said his work crew, under orders from the Serbs, also plundered the houses of displaced Muslims and loaded appliances and other possessions into trucks and took them to two warehouses in Prijedor.

Many of the prisoners who arrived here from Trnopolje had been incarcerated previously in Kereterm, a tile factory in the city of Prijedor, or in Omarska, an iron mine on the road between Prijedor and Banja Luka. After an international outcry following *Newsday*'s August 2 report on mass killings in the camps, Bosnian Serb authorities closed Kereterm and Omarska and transferred all the prisoners to Trnopolje. Their transfer to Croatia was the result of lengthy negotiations between the International Red Cross and the Bosnian Serb authorities, who promised during peace talks in London in August to close down the camps. Aside from scattered individual releases and a handful of escapes, this is the first large contingent to be released from the Serb camps.

After the physical and psychological traumas, the former detainees now face yet another—where to go. According to Peter Kessler, a spokesman for the UN High Commissioner for Refugees, "not one country has yet come forward to offer refuge" to them. Croatia, packed with refugees, will let them stay only two weeks. If foreign countries do not quickly offer to resettle the former inmates, the 3,500 men held at the Manjaca camp, also in northern Bosnia, cannot be released, Kessler said. Officials of the International Red Cross estimated last month that the Serbs were holding between 20,000 and 40,000 civilians in camps.

Accounts of survivors suggest that thousands died in the three camps in northwest Bosnia alone. At each location a pattern developed: During the nights the guards removed a number of prisoners who were never seen again.

Admir Krajisnik, 21, said he had been held at the vast Omarska complex in a small office building nicknamed the "White House." Each night, he said, guards would call out five to 10 men and take them away. "In the morning we would go out and see four or five bodies laid out on the grass," he recalled. The other men were never seen again.

Besim Javor, 49, was held at Trnopolje from June through September and recounted nights when guards seized five, eight or more men who then never returned. The most recent occasion was September 21, he said, when five people were taken away.

Then there were times when "a Serb acquaintance would come and call for a prisoner, take him out and kill him. One night, eight people were killed like that," he said. Many of the prisoners were buried in the backyards of houses near the camp, he said.

At Kereterm, the authorities removed five to six people each night, Kaltak said. He recalled that guards would ask prisoners to give their professions, "and if they found someone with a high position or a higher educational degree, they would execute him. I think the intelligentsia of Prijedor has just disappeared," he said.

In other instances described by the witnesses, the Serb security forces chose victims almost at random.

Dzenanovic, the man who had no family to greet him here, said he lived in Gareci, a mainly Serb village south of Prijedor, in the first house at the entrance of the village. "They did the same thing to the family who lived in the last house in the village, which was also owned by a Muslim," he said. Besides his family, he lost all his property. "They took my car, my two cows, they stole the hay and the firewood, stripped everything from my house down to the doors and window frames," he said.

Many Muslims have expressed surprise over the degree to which neighbors and friends took part in the repression of non-Serbs.

When Kaltak reached Trnopolje on August 13, he discovered that the camp director was Slobodan Kuruzovic, his former elementary school principal from Prijedor. During daylight hours when Kuruzovic was there, he took an interest in the prisoners and treated many with kindness, Kaltak said. The terror began at night, after he had left.

On Thursday, as the detainees piled into 34 buses, Kaltak related, Kuruzovic was on hand to say good-bye. "All my pupils are going," Kuruzovic said.

A Muslim prisoner corrected him. "You mean your martyrs," he said.

❖

Death Camp Horrors
The Killing Went on Almost Everywhere

Omarska, Bosnia-Herzegovina, October 18, 1992

The vast mining complex here, with its open pits and ore processing system, looks like anything but a concentration camp. The nondescript buildings in their barren frontier landscape have been cleaned up, and there is no trace of the blood reputedly spilled here. But during the last month dozens of eyewitnesses have provided compelling new evidence of murder and torture on a wide scale at this complex, where the Serbs who conquered Bosnia brought several thousand Muslims and Croats to die.

According to former detainees, the killing went on almost everywhere: Inside the huge hangarlike building that houses earth-moving equipment, armed guards ordered excruciating tortures at gunpoint, sometimes forcing one prisoner to castrate another. The tarmac outside was an open-air prison where 500 to 1,000 men had to lie on their bellies from dawn to dusk. Thousands more packed the offices, workshops and storage rooms in the hangar and a glass-and-brick administration building. All were on starvation diets.

The two most-feared locations were small outbuildings some distance from the main facilities: the "Red House," from which no prisoner returned alive, and the "White House," which contained a torture chamber where guards beat prisoners for days until they succumbed.

Unlike Nazi concentration camps, Omarska kept no real records, making it extremely difficult to determine exactly how many died. Guards often chose victims at whim and had to ask other detainees to identify the corpses. "They never knew how many people were killed from one shift to the next," observed a 22-year-old Omarska survivor who asked that his name not be used.

Newsday first reported mass murders at Omarska and other camps on August 2. Five days later, as television pictures of emaciated prisoners were aired worldwide, Serb authorities closed the camp and dispersed the prisoners. But not until hundreds of survivors reached the West in the last few weeks, aided by the International Red Cross, was it possible to draw up a detailed account.

A month-long *Newsday* investigation, which included extensive interviews with officials who said they were responsible for Omarska and with dozens of former detainees in Croatia, Britain and Bosnia itself, produced these main conclusions:

- Eyewitness accounts of detainees indicate that well over 1,000 people were killed at Omarska, and thousands more probably would have died of beatings, executions, disease or starvation had the camp not been closed.
- A large number of detainees, possibly as many as 1,000, seem to have disappeared without a trace when the camp was closed.
- All but a few detainees were civilians, mostly draft-age Muslim or Croat men, but there were many men under 18 or over 60, and a small number of women.

Newsday's estimate of the death toll of more than 1,000 is based on eyewitness accounts of daily killings by three former detainees who spoke in separate interviews. It does not reflect other, possibly duplicative, first-person reports of mass executions or disappearances; if it did, the toll could easily be twice as high.

Three Bosnian journalists who were detained at Omarska and are now being held in another camp arrived among themselves at an estimated death toll of 1,200 or more. And International Red Cross officials said at least 2,000 people who went to Omarska are unaccounted for.

Nine hundred miles from here, outside London, Edin Elkaz lies awake nights, his head filled with the screams of the men being tortured in the room next door at the White House. During one month at the camp, the 21-year-old said, he witnessed some of the killings next door and the removal of bodies the next day; the guards slaughtered five to 10 men a night, up to 30 on some nights. The guards sang as they beat the Muslim and Croat prisoners to death, sometimes nationalist songs about "Greater Serbia," other times religious melodies from the Serb Orthodox liturgy, he said. E.L., a 26-year-old Muslim, spent two months here and said he helped load between five and 10 corpses daily from the White House into a small yellow pickup truck that removed them to an unknown grave. Like many of those interviewed, he asked that his full name not be used.

And N.J., a 23-year-old Muslim, said he kept a count each night for the final 20 nights of the inmates marched to the Red House. Some days there were as few as 17 or as many as 42. None ever returned.

Interviews with these three detainees, who are among 68 taken to Britain to recover from beatings and shootings, and from several hundred who recently arrived in Karlovac, western Croatia, provide chilling amplification of the original reports of atrocities at the camps in Bosnia.

Reacting to the early accounts, Lawrence Eagleburger, now the acting U.S. secretary of state, said on August 18 that the administration had found no evidence of systematic killing, only of unpleasant conditions. But after conducting its own interviews recently with about 40 former detainees in Karlovac for submission to a special United Nations war crimes panel, the United States Embassy in Zagreb has concluded there were massive atrocities at Omarska and other camps and in the surrounding towns, said an embassy official.

"The Nazis had nothing on these guys. I've seen reports of individual acts of barbarity of a kind that hasn't come up in State Department cable traffic in 20 years," said another top official at the U.S. embassy, who spoke on condition of anonymity.

But even the United States Embassy interviewers have been unable to determine the number of people held at Omarska, the number killed or the number missing.

Extensive *Newsday* interviews with prisoners indicate that at least 2,500 to 3,000 detainees were held in Omarska at any one point. International Red Cross officials have a working estimate that up to 5,000 prisoners were taken to Omarska and that well over 2,000 are accounted for.

Despite the imprecision of the statistics, the story of Omarska and other concentration camps in Bosnia constitutes one of the most savage chapters of modern European history. Serbs from nearby Prijedor set up camps at Omarska and Kereterm, a disused tile factory, on May 25, not quite a month after they seized power by force in the town of 30,000. Officials from Prijedor were eager to present their version of events but acknowledged under questioning by *Newsday* that it was only the official account. "You have your facts. We have our facts. You have a complete right to choose between the two versions," police chief Simo Drljaca said in an interview last month.

Almost nothing in the official version stands up to scrutiny.

During a tour of the administration building at the camp, Zeljko Mejahic, the former commander of the guards, took a visitor to a basement room packed with rows of bunk beds. There were never more than 270 prisoners at Omarska at any one time, Mejahic said, "and this is where they all slept."

But the detainees said they had slept on the ground, on floors or crouching jammed into closets—anywhere but in beds. The beds were brought a few days after the media drew attention to Omarska, according to a foreign humanitarian aid expert. The authorities raided military barracks for the bunks and the hotels of Banja Luka for the bedding, he said. Only when the bunks were in place were the International Red Cross and reporters allowed to visit.

Milan Kovacevic, the city manager in Prijedor, said Omarska was an investigative facility, set up "to see who did what during the war, to find the guilty ones and to establish the innocent so that they didn't bear the consequences." He said the camp was closed when the investigation was completed.

Drljaca, a little-known law graduate who became police chief when the Serb minority took power, said 3,334 people were arrested on suspicion of resisting or plotting against the new Serb authorities and were taken to Omarska. Drljaca insisted that no one had been killed at Omarska and that only two prisoners died between May 25 and mid-August, both of "natural causes." Another 49 "disappeared," including the former lord mayor of Prijedor, Mohamed Cehajic, and were presumed dead, Drljaca said.

In the official version, detainees were interrogated for four days and shipped out. Drljaca said 800 detainees who were alleged to have "organized the whole thing," among them rich Muslims who financed the Muslim SDA political party, were taken to Manjaca, which was operated by the Bosnian Serb army as a prisoner-of-war camp, to await criminal trial. Taken with them were 600 people who reputedly commanded units of the Muslim and Croat resistance. The remaining 1,900 were found innocent and taken immediately to Trnopolje, which officials said was a transit camp, Drljaca said.

But not one of more than three dozen Omarska survivors whom U.S. embassy officials interviewed at Karlovac said he had been questioned before being taken to Omarska. Only a few of several dozen interviewed by *Newsday* had been interrogated, and they said they were beaten before and during questioning. Most had been held more than two months.

Moreover, nearly every Omarska prisoner sent to

Manjaca was a civilian, and only a handful had borne arms against the Serbs—nowhere near the 600 figure given by Drljaca, humanitarian aid sources say.

Drljaca's assertion that prisoners were removed to Manjaca after being interrogated was contradicted by Bozidor Popovic, the commander at Manjaca, who said in an interview last month that 25 busloads of prisoners had arrived in early August.

Slobodan Balaban, an ethnic Serb who was technical director of the mining complex, said Serbs were motivated to operate the camps by revenge for the perceived suffering of Serbs in other conflicts. "The main factor that influenced our conduct has been the treatment of our people who were taken to Croatian camps," he said.

While official accounts are riddled with contradictions, reports by survivors of Omarska of severe deprivation, brutal tortures and routinized slaughter are consistent and corroborative, as well as mind-numbing. According to the reports, some of which follow, savagery enveloped the prisoners from their arrival.

Redzep Tahirovic, 52, said he was brought to Omarska with hundreds of others on May 26 after Serbs destroyed and "cleansed" the nearby Muslim town of Kozarac. In a sworn statement given to the Bosnian State Commission on War Crimes, he said guards called out a dozen people a day for five days and decapitated them with chain saws near one of the main pits. He said Omarska prisoners were forced to witness the massacre as well as the subsequent execution of 20 non-Serb policemen from Prijedor.

D.K., a 25-year-old ethnic Albanian now recovering outside London, had the luck to be shot by accident on arriving at Omarska on May 30. "I was there only 20 minutes," he said. He had been among 15 men standing near the camp entrance who were fired at by a trigger-happy guard. D.K. lifted his pajamas to show seven bullet wounds on his stomach, legs and arm. Three detainees died in the shooting, but

D.K. was taken to a hospital in Banja Luka where he was in a coma for 15 days. When he came to, he said, nurses, Serb patients and even Serb children visitors came and beat him. "I had gotten 12 pints of blood, and they beat me because I had Serb blood," he said.

Edin Elkaz was also lucky to be shot by accident on arrival May 30 and taken to a hospital in Prijedor, for it reduced his exposure to the violence in the camp. Elkaz had been a Bosnian soldier, one of the few Omarska prisoners who had actually fought the Serbs. Stuffed with 130 others into a one-car garage, Elkaz was standing near the door when guards seized a friend of his and executed him outside at close range.

The bullet penetrated the door, entered the stomach of Elkaz's brother and finally came to rest in Elkaz's leg. In the hospital for six weeks with his leg suspended from a bar, Elkaz never recovered because Serb ill-wishers came by and poked the wound with a stick, repeatedly reinfecting it.

"I had a very good [Serb] neighbor who came by one day and said hello. I came to regret it," Elkaz said, smiling at the irony. "He brought 15 people to beat me up over six weeks."

Once back in Omarska, he was taken with several other Bosnian soldiers to a room in the "White House." He could see the beatings through a glass door. The guards used wooden clubs and iron bars and usually concentrated on the head, the genitals, the spine and the kidneys. Sometimes they smashed prisoners' heads against radiators. "You'd see pieces of flesh or brain there the next day," Elkaz recalled.

But the worst torture was to stand a prisoner against the wall and beat him with a cable. "I think they killed at least 50 men with that cable," Elkaz said.

Each morning, he said, detainees laid out the corpses on the tarmac in front of the White House. Others then loaded them into the small yellow truck that had just been used to deliver food to the camp kitchen. A four-man burial detail would accompany the truck, but only one would return alive.

No prisoner is known to have survived the "Red House," and only a few even witnessed detainees being taken each night to the outbuilding, well away from the main buildings. From mid-July until Omarska was closed, starting at 8 each night, guards collected men from different locations in the camp and took them to a holding area at the White House, according to the former detainee, N.J. Guards asked them for names and family details, then marched them away individually. At about 4 A.M. prisoners would hear a truck drive up to the Red House, apparently to collect the corpses.

Although guards often combed the many rooms where prisoners were kept and called out names from lists, many of those killed or beaten were selected at random. "The guards would come in at 3 A.M. and take five people out, telling us they were going to be exchanged. Where they took them, God only knows," said M.M., a 28-year-old plumber held with more than 500 men for more than two months in a room adjacent to the giant hangar. "Next morning we would see the dead bodies. I am sure that 50 percent of those who disappeared would be killed."

Often the guards did not know whom they had beaten to death. Elkaz recalled that "sometimes they would call them by name. But sometimes they would ask me afterward, 'Do you know who this is?'" He said he identified many friends who had been beaten to death.

The violence worsened in time as the guards "had already taken everything of value," said a man who called himself by the pseudonym Mrki, aged 40, interviewed at Karlovac. Mrki was taken to the White House because he was standing in a prominent location when a guard came into the room looking for scapegoats. Over two nights, he was beaten unconscious at the White House, both by guards and by villagers invited in for recreational beating. "When I awoke in the morning, there was blood all over the place," he recalled.

There were ways to avoid beatings, detainees said. Rule

one was never to look a guard in the eye. Rule two was that if called to an interrogation, to confuse the guards by saying you had just come from one. Prisoners sometimes smeared themselves with blood from a newly beaten detainee "so that we would be spared as much as possible in the next round," Kamber Midho, 31, said in a sworn statement to the Bosnian government. At least one prisoner was burned alive at Omarska.

The burning occurred in late July as detainees lined up for lunch, according to Nedjad Hadzic, 23, an eyewitness now in Karlovac. The man was emerging from an interrogation, and a guard ordered him to run, as if in preparation to shoot him. "You are cowards. You know nothing but cruelty," the man taunted the guard.

When the guards were shoving him on the tarmac, he grabbed a gun from one of them but then gave it up. "They shoved him toward the White House, poured gasoline over him and set him alight," Hadzic said.

And Osman Hamuric, who is now recovering outside London, told Newsday he had twice witnessed forced cannibalism at Kereterm camp. On one occasion, he said, guards cut off a prisoner's ear and forced another man to eat it. The second time, a guard cut a piece of flesh off a wounded prisoner and told him to eat it. He refused. "Why not? It's cooked," Hamuric quoted the guard as saying. Hamuric could not say whether the man ate his own flesh. "All I know is that they took him away, and we never saw him again."

Yet nothing was more traumatic for the men than the castrations. United States Embassy officials found a witness to an incident in which a man had his testicles tied with wire to the back of a motorcycle, which took off at high speed. He died of massive blood loss.

Hadzic described a castration in an interview with *Newsday*. The incident began when a guard with a grudge to settle called out Emir Karabasic, a Muslim policeman, from the room in which Hadzic was sleeping and ordered him to strip naked in the hangar in front of parked dump trucks. "Do you remember the time you beat me up in the cafe?" the guard asked. As Hadzic watched from the next room, a second Serb policeman found another Muslim, against whose father he had a grudge, and ordered him to lower his face into a channel cut in the concrete floor and drink old motor oil, then to bite off Karabasic's testicles. "The shrieks were unbearable. Then there was silence," said Hadzic.

Three other men who had been removed from Hadzic's room at the same time and witnessed the castration were then killed by the guards with metal rods, Hadzic said. The man who carried out the castration returned to the room, his face blackened, and could not speak for 24 hours.

Experiences like these have left deep psychic scars on the survivors, among them a Roman Catholic priest from near Prijedor who described his suffering to parishioners in Zagreb. The priest, who spoke briefly with *Newsday* but insisted he not be identified, told them he had been beaten until he vomited blood. Once he said he had been caught trying to give a detainee the last rites, and he swallowed the piece of bread he had consecrated rather than let the guards seize it.

From dawn to dusk he lay out on the tarmac with hundreds of other men. For 32 days, the priest said, he did not have a bowel movement because he had not eaten any food. "It was so terrible that, God forgive me for saying so, we were grateful when someone died. We could take their clothing and place it under us," an attendee at his speech quoted him as saying. The ordeal caused damage to the priest's heart and kidneys, and he is now recovering in Croatia.

During their first five days in Omarska, prisoners were generally given no food, witnesses said. After that time they were taken in groups of 30 to the cafeteria for the sole meal of the day, which consisted of a slice of bread and a bowl of thin soup. After two or three minutes, during which it was possible to wolf down a few spoonfuls of the gruel, it was back to the tarmac.

The beatings that accompanied trips to the toilet were so severe that former detainees said they preferred to defecate in their boots or in the rooms in which they had to sleep. Dysentery was rampant, and conditions were so unclean that some prisoners counted 10 types of lice or vermin on their bodies. "We had lice on our eyelids. They'd fall out of our beards," said Hadzic. Detainees said they bathed only twice all summer. The guards ordered prisoners to disrobe in groups of 50 and then aimed fire hoses at their genitals. "It was pure sadism. They'd laugh if we fell over," Hadzic said.

When Omarska was closed down, camp doctors at Manjaca estimated that of the prisoners transferred there, at least one in 10 had contracted dysentery from bad food or unsanitary conditions, all of whom would have succumbed without immediate treatment. Others suffered from untreated and festering wounds from their beatings.

Many others were close to collapse. "I don't believe I would have lasted another 10 days," said Kemal Husic, 19. "I was reaching a state where I couldn't stand. I had to have two people help me to get to the cafeteria."

Hadzic concurred. "There was so much hunger and dysentery that the whole camp couldn't have lasted another 20 days," he said.

Many detainees never made it to safety and seem to have disappeared "in transit" to or from Omarska. These included two busloads of men who disappeared from Omarska at the end of July. Another 120, according to witnesses, were to be taken from the Kereterm camp to Omarska on August 5 but never turned up. About 11 men who were transferred to Manjaca did not arrive. Guards slit the throats of two and killed another nine, prisoners said.

The Manjaca commander, Bozidor Popovic, disclaimed

any knowledge of that alleged atrocity. "I am not interested in what happened outside the gates. My responsibility is only for what happens under my control."

But the biggest mystery is what happened to the people transferred from Omarska at the time of its closing. Prisoners said they reckoned a population of 2,500 to 3,000 at Omarska, basing their estimates on such things as counts of the lunches served on a particular day. Of the prisoners there at the end, 1,374 were transferred to Manjaca, according to the International Red Cross. About 700 others went to Trnopolje, according to prisoners later taken from there to Karlovac. That leaves between 500 and 1,000 missing. Moreover, of the number transferred to Trnopolje in early August, only about 200 made it to Karlovac. Some had been on a convoy into central Bosnia in which more than 250 men were slaughtered by local police.

Were other Omarska prisoners killed in other ways? Were they dispersed to other camps? No one has an answer, not even Thierry Germond, the chief European delegate for the International Red Cross, which has tried to win freedom for all the civilian and military detainees in the war. All Germond could say was, "We understand your concern, and I share it."

❖

Nowhere to Go

Slow Reaction to Biggest Refugee Crisis Since World War II

Zagreb, Croatia, November 1, 1992

In a shabby campsite on the outskirts of town, Semina Karagic clutched her sickly 4-year-old son while a relative carefully replaced a blanket over the open door frame. Eighteen Bosnian Muslims huddled on blankets on the floor of the former laborers' dormitory, which lacked beds, heat, running water and sanitary facilities. A visiting doctor said the camp was one step away from a hepatitis epidemic.

"It's cold now for us grownups. You can imagine what it's like for the young," said the 41-year-old woman, who went overnight from her own two-story home "with all the appliances" to a life of abject poverty.

But Karagic and 5,000 others at the Resnik camp 10 days ago are the lucky ones. They got out before Croatia closed its borders in July to Bosnian refugees, including women and children. Hundreds of thousands of countrymen trapped in the terror and mayhem of Serb "ethnic cleansing" in northern Bosnia would give anything to be in their place.

"These people have absolutely nowhere to go. They will get killed if they stay where they are, or starve or be exposed to freezing temperatures. Or they can take a perilous trek across battlefields to central Bosnia, which also has blown up," said Manda Na-Champassak, a spokeswoman for the UN High Commissioner for Refugees.

The prospects for Bosnians seeking refuge dimmed further recently when Zagreb abandoned its alliance with Bosnia-Herzegovina and joined Serbia to call for a carving up of the predominantly Muslim republic. The collapse of the alliance allowed Serbia to capture the Bosnian stronghold of Jajce last week, and thousands of mostly Muslim refugees are fleeing the city under shelling by the Serbs.

Croatia's decision to deny refuge to the Bosnians is a blatant violation of the right to seek asylum from persecution stated in the 1948 Universal Declaration of Human Rights, but it has evoked only the mildest of protests. "If we criticize Croatia, they might send the Muslims back to Bosnia," explained an official of one international aid group who asked not to be identified. The official noted that Croatia has taken in well over 300,000 Bosnian refugees, perhaps as many as all the rest of Europe. "It's really hard to criticize the Croats. All their hotels, gymnasia and schools are full of refugees."

A New York *Newsday* survey of refugee policy in the United States and seven European countries suggests another reason for the muted reaction. Governments from Britain to Italy can claim their borders are open to Bosnian refugees, fully aware that with Croatia blocking their exit, almost none can get out. Croatia's action has shielded Europe from the full impact of its biggest refugee crisis since World War II.

Former Polish Prime Minister Tadeusz Mazowiecki, who heads a United Nations human rights investigation in Bosnia, criticized Croatia and even the UN military force guarding key Bosnian-Croatian crossings for turning away many displaced Muslims and rounding up and returning draft-age men. "The majority of displaced persons can only save their lives by seeking refuge outside the borders of Bosnia and Herzegovina," he said in a report last week. But the High Commissioner for Refugees, while issuing repeated warnings of impending catastrophe, is making no attempt to find places abroad for refugees, putting all its efforts into delivering food into central Bosnia.

"Look, we can't even find slots for those few thousand

traumatized men who were in prison camps, death camps," said Sylvana Foa, the chief spokeswoman for the commissioner for refugees. "All we get are symbolic gestures from countries who demanded the camps be closed—50 here, 100 there. Imagine what we would find if we asked for places for two million people. And we have two million people who we consider at serious risk. There is no way we can ask the world to take two million people."

The nonpartisan U.S. Committee for Refugees said in a report last week that the Bosnian crisis has become a challenge to basic Western values. "What happened at Croatia's border represents a fundamental breakdown in the principle of first asylum, a system of burden sharing whereby governments distant from a conflict assist countries in the immediate vicinity to permit them to offer at least temporary asylum to give refugees some immediate escape route when their lives are threatened," the report said.

Both the UN High Commissioner for Refugees and the International Red Cross say money is no problem. What is lacking, they say, is determination even to implement repeated Security Council resolutions pledging to ensure the safe delivery of relief supplies.

The doors began closing for Bosnians just as eyewitness accounts began to surface of the massive atrocities they had suffered. Germany, the traditional first choice of asylum seekers in Europe, which counts 220,000 refugees from the former Yugoslavia, mostly from Croatia, imposed a visa requirement in May, shortly after Serb forces invaded Bosnia. Early in July, as the government of Serbia began expelling Bosnian refugees to other countries, Austria imposed a visa obligation on passports issued by the Serbian authorities. Hungary and the former Yugoslav republic of Slovenia effectively closed their borders. A few weeks later Croatia followed suit.

The United States has not taken a leading role in upholding the right of refuge. "Our sense is that it is better to have countries take the refugees who are closer to Bosnia," said a senior State Department official who spoke on condition of anonymity. "We want to find first asylum as close as possible to home on the assumption that one day they should be allowed to return home." He acknowledged that "there is a possible reality out there that maybe Serbia will control Bosnia in a more or less permanent way" and that the refugees will never be able to return. "Then you have an enormous problem."

After repeated pleas by the UN High Commissioner for Refugees and the Swiss-based International Red Cross, the United States agreed last week to give refuge to 1,000 Bosnians. These are to be some of the 1,561 former detainees in Serb-run concentration camps who have been in Karlovac, Croatia, for the last month awaiting placement, and their families. This could amount to as few as 250 of the detainees.

Enough countries have finally come forward to accommodate all of the 1,561 former detainees, but the offers fall far short of the 3,000 to 5,000 additional former camp detainees who are about to be released. No country seems prepared to accept large numbers of other refugees.

Aside from Croatia and Slovenia, which refuse to take additional refugees, the only country of first refuge for Bosnians is Italy, which has only a maritime boundary with Bosnia by virtue of the republic's short stretch of Adriatic seacoast. "We are accepting as many as we can of those who succeed to get out," said Antonio Cavaterra, who is in charge of refugee admissions at the Italian Interior Ministry.

But Italy has only 2,000 to 3,000 refugees in addition to about 17,000 Bosnians staying with friends or family. The reason, aid experts say, is that although Italy says letters of invitation are unnecessary for admission, no Bosnian can cross Croatia or Slovenia without those letters. Italy also declines to send buses or trains into Croatia or Bosnia to pick up refugees.

In Slovenia, which has 69,000 refugees and refuses passage to anyone without papers for a third country, Joze Pucnik, vice president of the Slovene government, scoffed at the Italian claim of open borders. He said Italy avoids taking refugees "largely through cute bureaucratic tricks." Several Slovene officials, asked if they thought Italy would accept busloads of refugees if they arrived at the Italian border, scoffed. "No way," said one.

A Bosnian representative in Ljubljana, the Slovenian capital, who asked not to be named, said he had been negotiating with Spain to send 300 refugees there, but when he reached the point of requesting a group visa and letter, "the lines went dead. I haven't heard from them for the past month," he said.

Austria, which says it has 65,000 Bosnians and has no visa requirement for Bosnians, refuses to accept any who have spent more than two weeks in another country, a common practice that eliminates many refugees.. "We get 40 to 50 refugees a day, which is what we can manage," said an official in the refugee affairs division. But he noted that for the past month or so Austria has "seen no people coming any more directly from the war region."

Hungary, which received 50,000 Croatian refugees in 1991 after the Serb-led Yugoslav army attacked Croatia, has only about 4,000 Bosnians. It has not imposed a visa requirement but turns away those without transit visas and does not admit any "except those who are really refugees and in a desperate situation," said Janos Herman, an immigration official. "It is a huge problem. We need a broader, international effort," he said.

Britain and France both say they have imposed no limits on Bosnians entering their countries, although the number who have sought asylum is 4,000 and 1,108 respectively. British authorities say 35,000 people from the former

Yugoslavia have arrived since January as "visitors" but had no breakdown regarding Bosnian Muslims.

The French government, which says it has no exact figures, is reluctant to take in even former detainees. Unlike most countries, according to UNHCR officials, the French government says it fears that accepting too many refugees would pose a security risk.

Hans Joerg Eiff, a former German ambassador to Yugoslavia who now heads his country's refugee efforts, deplores the complacent attitude about the refugees. "I have been telling my people for weeks that we are facing a huge catastrophe," he said. "Tens of thousands will try to get out. Many will try to make their way here." But in Germany, as elsewhere, the focus remains on domestic politics.

"Nobody really accepts what is happening," said Na-Champassak of the UNHCR. "Nobody wants to believe it is happening. Not until you see images of frozen bodies scattered in the hundreds will people react. Then there will be total outrage."

OUT IN THE COLD

An estimate of the number of displaced people and refugees from Bosnia-Herzegovina within the former Yugoslavia.

Present Location	Estimate
Bosnia-Herzegovina	740,000
Croatia	336,671
Serbia	267,693
Slovenia	69,000
Montenegro	54,484
Macedonia	28,800
Total	1,496,648

Note: Total does not include some 760,000 people in besieged central Bosnia. There are also an estimated 592,416 displaced Croatians within the former Yugoslavia.

LIVING IN OTHER COUNTRIES

An estimate of the number of refugees from the former Yugoslavia living in other selected countries.

Present Location	Estimate
Austria	65,000
Britain	4,000
France	1,108
Germany	220,000
Hungary	54,000
Italy	3,000
Sweden	67,465
Switzerland	70,450

Source: UN High Commissioner for Refugees, individual countries.

Death Camp Lists

In Town after Town, Bosnia's Elite "Disappeared"

Omarska, Bosnia-Herzegovina, Sunday, November 8, 1992

The Serb guards strode menacingly into the crowded basement room in the middle of the night and called out the names of seven men. It was a virtual *Who's Who* of leading Muslims and Croats from nearby Prijedor: Muhamed Cehajic, the elected lord mayor of the city of 112,000; two gynecologists at the Prijedor hospital; the owner of a cafe and art gallery; a state prosecutor; and two others. Aside from one Croat, all were Muslims.

One by one, they rose from the corrugated cardboard and rags on which they slept in the administration building of the mine complex-turned-concentration camp. They were led away by the guards and never again seen alive. Several eyewitnesses reported seeing and identifying the corpses of the seven men in a nearby field the next day. The witnesses, who are among the 10,000 or more former Omarska detainees waiting in Serb prisons for a Western country to offer refuge, spoke on condition of anonymity.

Over two days, July 26 and 27, the Serbs called about 50 people, according to witnesses, and they included judges, businessmen, teachers, surgeons, and civil servants—"all the prominent people of Prijedor," in the words of one ex-detainee.

With their disappearance, Prijedor's power structure was virtually eliminated, a graphic example of the deliberate destruction of the non-Serb elite that was an apparent war aim of the military juggernaut the Serbs rolled across Bosnia.

"It seems as if everything happening to me is as in an ugly

dream, a nightmare," Cehajic had written his family from a Banja Luka jail six weeks earlier. "I keep wondering whom and how much I have offended so that I have to go through all of this. . . . It is inconceivable to me that all of this is happening to us. Is life so unpredictable and so brutal?"

It is a question asked repeatedly by the 2 million Muslims of Bosnia-Herzegovina as they witness the systematic destruction of their people, their land, their economy and their 500-year-old culture. Methods differed from town to town, but the underlying pattern, according to extensive interviews with refugees and Bosnian police, was to round up the wealthiest, the most educated, the most successful, and the political and religious leadership from previously prepared lists.

In mostly Muslim eastern Bosnia, Serb paramilitary forces reportedly executed them in their villages. In some conquered areas of northern Bosnia, they took them to camps where they were executed without any judicial proceedings. But in northwestern Bosnia, a mainly Serb area including Prijedor, there are signs of a power struggle between the Serbs long entrenched in power, who favored judicial proceedings, and radicals, who preferred summary executions. The latter group apparently carried the day.

"They killed the judges, teachers, the president of the court, company directors, the wealthy—all the prominent people at Omarska," said one former Omarska detainee, a 40-year-old professional man.

Cehajic's daughter, Amira, compiled a list of 59 names of well-known Prijedor residents who reportedly had been taken to Omarska. After she fled to Zagreb, Croatia, in late July, she gave a copy to *Newsday* in the hope that publicity might lead to the release of all the prisoners, including her father. Unbeknownst to her, Cehajic had apparently died two days earlier.

Prijedor's lord mayor was one of those caught in the power struggle over the detainees. Ousted by Serbs in a military coup on April 29 and arrested on May 23, Cehajic was transferred back and forth between concentration camps and jail, and the Serbs seemed unable to decide how to deal with him. On August 18, nearly three weeks after his reported death, a court in Prijedor formally announced that he had been charged with the criminal offense of resisting the armed forces but said it had turned his case over to a military court.

Serb officials give vague and varying accounts of what happened to Cehajic and the dozens of other Prijedor men. In the first of two *Newsday* interviews in September, Simo Drljaca, a law graduate who rose from obscurity to become police chief in Prijedor after the Serb coup, said Cehajic was among 49 inmates who "escaped" from the camp in northern Bosnia. His followers organized his escape from Omarska, Drljaca asserted in the presence of his superior, Stojan Zupljanin, the Serb chief of security for the Banja Luka region.

A week later, on his home turf in Prijedor, he put it more bluntly. Cehajic, who was 53 at the time, had "disappeared." "You know how it is. You find they disappeared," said Drljaca. "There may be some who died in the process of disappearing."

Drljaca later escorted a Newsday reporter on a tour of Omarska and listened as Zeljko Mejahic, the former commander of the guards at the camp, recited the official explanation: "There was a power cut at 11:47 P.M. on July 26, and it lasted until 4:30 A.M. the next morning." Cehajic "disappeared among seven who left at that time."

Former detainees at Omarska have said without exception that no one, in fact, ever escaped the camp, which was at the edge of a Serbian mining village. Drljaca had a ready answer for that contention. "People got out of Alcatraz," he said.

Cehajic, who spent his adult life as a high school teacher, had had no involvement in politics until 1990, when he decided to join the newly formed Muslim Party of Democratic Action and run for office.

"I urged him not to join the party. I said there was no future for ethnic parties," recalled his wife Minka, 54, a pediatrician and the former director of the Prijedor hospital, who is now living in Zagreb. But Cehajic would not be stopped. "He said this would be a civil party, a middle-class party. He told us, 'All my life I've done everything out of love for you. If you don't like it, you should make a sacrifice this time,'" she said.

In the first elections of the post-communist era, Muslims, comprising 44 percent of the population of Prijedor, voted as a bloc for the party. Serbs, who composed 42 percent, were divided, with the radical nationalist Serbian Democratic Party taking 28 percent, and a more moderate party associated with then-federal prime minister Ante Markovic taking the rest of the vote. Cehajic became mayor, and Milomir Stahic, a member of the Serbian party, became his deputy.

Cehajic first ran up against Serb power in mid-1991 when the Serb-led Banja Luka corps of the Yugoslav army announced a general mobilization and began drafting men to join in the war against secessionist Croatia. "My father strongly opposed this and as a pacifist put himself on the side of all Croats, Muslims, and Serbs who did not want to take part in that war," recalled Amira, 27, who, like her mother, is a pediatrician. Cehajic's son, Amir, 20, is a medical student in Zagreb.

Cehajic's stand won him sympathy among Croats, but the Serbs never forgave him. In February of this year, after the United States and western Europe recognized Croatia, the predominantly Muslim government of Bosnia-Herzegovina held a referendum on independence from Yugoslavia. Muslims and Croats, who together comprise 61 percent of the republic's population, voted in favor, but Serb leader Radovan Karadjic declared an independent Serb state within Bosnia.

Backed by material aid and manpower from Serbia and the enormous arms and ammunition stockpile, military bases and command structure taken over from the Yugoslav army, Bosnian Serb forces launched a massive military offensive.

In Prijedor the Serb police and army forces took over the city hall and police station and ousted the Muslims. "We took power by force," Drljaca said matter-of-factly. "We took power with guns." He was especially pleased to note that Serbs from the left, who had voted against the Serbian party in the elections, "have now joined us."

Drljaca's justifications for the coup range from the self-serving to the bizarre. "We have proof that they were planning to do the same thing to us two days later," he said of the Muslims. "If Prijedor had fallen, Banja Luka would have, too," he said, speaking of the main regional city with twice the population. The only proof cited by the Serbs is a list purporting to show about 3,000 Muslims and Croats in the region had obtained small arms suitable for self-defense.

Another reason for ousting the coalition government was that Serbs had found "proof" the Muslims planned "to circumcise all Serb boys and kill all males over the age of 3, and send the women between the ages of 15 and 25 into a harem to produce janissaries," a reference to a Turkish medieval practice of forcing Serb women to bear children for use in the military. Asked for documentation, Drljaca said it was elsewhere in Bosnia.

Yet another reason was offered by Dragan Savanavic, a Serb who is the new deputy mayor of Prijedor. "Serbs can't allow a government in which they are a minority. Serbs in this area are a constitutive nation. They will never accept Izetbegovic as president." Alija Izetbegovic, a Muslim, is president of Bosnia.

Cehajic got in the way of the Serb view of political order. One day after the coup the new authorities ordered Cehajic to go on the radio and instruct the population to surrender all arms to the Serbs. Instead, "he called on the citizens to preserve the peace, to act with dignity and to conduct a Ghandian resistance to the illegal government," Minka Cehajic recalled.

Cehajic was suspended from his job but was free to move about until Serb police arrested him in his apartment on May 23 and charged him with organizing an attack on Serb soldiers in the nearby village of Hambarina the previous day. After his arrest other supposed charges began to pile up. Radio Prijedor, under Serb control, alleged that Cehajic was the son of a war criminal, a charge Drljaca repeated to *Newsday.* "In the last war, he took part in killing 6,000 Serbs. He was executed as a war criminal," he asserted about the father. It is a favorite charge by Serbs against Muslims, and its main relevance, a generation later, may be to motivate Serbs to seek revenge.

Cehajic's father, a baker, had been in the city government of Sanski Most during the World War II occupation by the Croatian Ustashe fascists, and shortly before the communist partisans entered the city, he disappeared. But according to Minka Cehajic, "Others who lived there said he had never dirtied his hands. He was never charged, and he was never tried." Cehajic was 5 at the time his father disappeared.

Drljaca also told *Newsday,* "We have data from at least 10 people who said Cehajic was advocating the war option for the Muslim people and fomented military preparations." Cehajic's wife said he was a pacifist who opposed the Muslims' taking up arms. "We were the apples of his eye. If he had known about an attack, he would have had us removed from Prijedor in advance," she said.

The more convincing reason offered for arresting him, however, was that he was there. "It's normal" to arrest the political leadership after a coup, Drljaca told *Newsday.*

Cehajic was first taken for interrogation to the police station, then to two detention camps the Serbs had set up in industrial sites, one at the Kereterm tile factory within the Prijedor city limits and the other at Omarska, a vast iron ore mining complex. He was jailed pending charges in Banja Luka from June 6 to June 20, and assigned a lawyer. Then he was returned to Omarska, where he was held for five weeks until July 26.

Few of the other men called out with Cehajic on those two fateful nights were politically active or even members of the Muslim party. Most were leaders in commerce, medicine or law.

One of the seven, Mehmetalija Kapitanovic, 48, a brother-in-law of Cehajic who headed a catering company, was arrested June 19. "I can't find any real connection between Meho and these other people who were arrested," his wife Sena told *Newsday*. The only possible connection, she said, was wealth or social prominence. "It seems they tortured the more eminent ones, whereas the ordinary, everyday people they would just kill," she said.

Osman Mahmuljan, a doctor specializing in internal medicine and about 47 years old, was also arrested in June on charges he had attempted to kill an ethnic Serb doctor by prescribing the wrong treatment after a heart attack.

Zeljko Sikora, a gynecologist, was arrested in mid-June and accused in the Serb-dominated media of sterilizing infant Serb boys at birth.

Asaf Kapitanovic, a cousin of Cehajic, was Prijedor's most prominent restaurateur and one of its wealthiest people. He had just gotten married, had opened a new cafe-art gallery and was building a new house when he was arrested in June.

The complete list of those called out with Cehajic is not known, but family members believe it also included Esad Mehmedagic, a public prosecutor about 55 years old, and Esad Sadikovic, the head of the ear, nose and throat department at the Prijedor hospital. Sadikovic had been indirectly involved in politics, having written a satirical political column in the newspaper in nearby Kozarac. But he had organized a peace demonstration in mid-1991 against the war in Croatia, and he was charged by the Serbs who arrested him as being a "false peace activist," according to Sena Kapitanovic.

The Serbs who run Prijedor today seem indifferent to the fate of the man they ousted from the job of mayor. When asked what happened to his predecessor, Stahic replied: "I don't know. He escaped." Later he added: "I would prefer to have him in jail so that tomorrow we could put him before the court in a proper trial or release him."

Milan Kovacevic, the city manager, joked that "there is even the chance he will call us from Paris. Or we can go to the other extreme, and he is among the dead. No one can say. There is more chance that he will phone from Paris or London than that you will exhume him dead."

Confronted with the assertion of eyewitnesses who saw Cehajic's corpse, Drljaca did not try to dispute it. "They have their version. We have ours. You have the complete right to choose between them," he said.

Of the 59 names on Amira Cehajic's list, Serb authorities confirmed to *Newsday* that 13 had "escaped" or "died in the process of disappearing."

No eyewitness has confirmed to their faces that their father and husband is dead, and the Cehajic women, who are both intelligent and self-assured, cling to the hope that he is still alive. His wife continues to hope he may have been taken elsewhere, citing the case of a Croatian friend whose husband, the president of the Prijedor court, was called out from Omarska and taken to another camp.

"We know that everyone else who 'disappeared' is dead," said Cehajic's daughter. "They were killed inside the camp. People saw their corpses."

Serb authorities closed the Omarska camp in the days after *Newsday* first reported that massive atrocities had occurred there, and they moved the surviving detainees to Trnopolje, which the Serbs describe as a transit camp, and Manjaca, which they call a prisoner-of-war camp.

A few days after Omarska prisoners arrived at Trnopolje,

Prijedor, Bosnia-Herzegovina: The men in charge of the Omarska death camp, city manager Milan Kovacevic and police chief Simo Drljaca. According to them, only two people died at Omarska, both of "natural causes." (Boris Geilert/GAFF)

Zeljko Mejahic, commander of the guard at Omarska, accused of torturing prisoners and raping Jadranka Cigelj, a woman attorney from Prijedor. He brushes aside all charges: "I would not lean a bicycle on her, let alone rape her." (Boris Geilert/GAFF)

Prijedor: Bosnian Serb police who conducted "investigations" at Omarska point to stacks of files as they discuss the fate of "disappeared" prisoners. (Boris Geilert/GAFF)

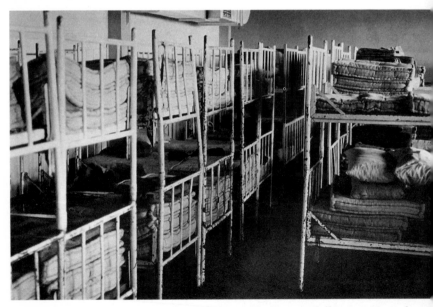

Omarska: After emptying the camp in early August following *Newsday* disclosures, authorities installed bunk beds and mattresses, then opened the facility to the press and other visitors. Officials say there were 270 prisoners and all slept in the beds; former prisoners say it was ten times that number and all slept on the floor. (Boris Geilert/GAFF)

Trnopolje, northern Bosnia: Serb authorities closed down the Omarska camp in August and shifted 1,571 prisoners to this schoolhouse detention camp. When places were found for them two months later, 3,500 refugees flocked to the site. But Europe's borders were shut and they languished for months. (Andree Kaiser/GAFF)

Manjaca: Most survivors of Omarska were taken to the army-run POW camp, where they were held on the floor of open cattle sheds from August until December. (Boris Geilert/GAFF)

Travnik: A Muslim refugee who escaped "ethnic cleansing" in north Bosnia. After abandoning their property and paying hundreds of dollars for transportation, refugees are dropped off after dusk at the top of Vlasic Mountain and told to walk more than a mile on a narrow cliffside road where armed men strip, rob and rape them, and sometimes push them over the precipice. (Andree Kaiser/GAFF)

Sarajevo: Ankica Sakota kneels beside the coffin of son Matej, 12 weeks old, who died for want of proper medical treatment at a Sarajevo hospital (Andree Kaiser/GAFF)

Sarajevo: Arrival of the wounded at a Kosovo hospital. (Andree Kaiser/GAFF)

Sarajevo: Pedestrians dash across a gap in the protective fence amid intense sniper fire. (Andree Kaiser/GAFF)

Sarajevo: A boy plays soldier until startled by a nearby blast. (Andree Kaiser/GAFF)

a middle-aged woman garbed in a scarf and old clothes boarded one of the rare trains from Prijedor to Trnopolje. It was Minka Cehajic. For an hour and a half she talked to prisoners who had seen her husband at Omarska, but they could give her no firm word of his fate. She walked the eight miles home, using an umbrella to conceal her face from Serb guards.

Shortly before she escaped from Prijedor, Minka Cehajic received from a newly released prisoner a letter her husband had written in early June. It is an intense and personal document, in which he expressed his love for the family, his hope that he would be freed and his gratitude that a friend had brought him cigarettes. "Thank him for eternity," he said. "If it hadn't been for that, I would have thought I was completely alone in the world."

He appealed to her to find him a new lawyer and send some cigarettes, more changes of underwear, a shaving set, a track suit and ground coffee.

The letter arrived weeks after Cehajic was last seen alive. Despite all the indications to the contrary, his wife and daughter hope that Cehajic is still alive. They want him to be vindicated.

"I would like my father to live for the day when the truth comes out," said Amira. "He was unjustly accused. But not just to live for this truth, but for the whole truth, because there were so many innocent people."

"I HAVE HEARD TERRIBLE THINGS"

Letter from Mohamed Cehajic, June 9, 1992:

My dear Minka: I am writing you this letter though I am not at all certain that you will get it. But still I feel the irrepressible need to talk with you in this way. Since that 23 May when they came to our house for me, I have been living in another world. It seems as if everything happening to me

is an ugly dream, a nightmare. And I simply cannot understand how something like this is possible, dear Minka,
Amira, and my son.

You know how much I love you, and because of this love
I have never done anything, nor could I do anything, that
could cause you pain. I know you know what they are trying
to put on me hasn't even a single part in the thousand of
connection with me. I keep wondering whom and how much
I have offended so that I have to go through all of this.

Nevertheless, I believe in justice and the truth, and this
will all be cleared up.

Otherwise, I think of you constantly, of your faces, which
are always before my eyes. I have to admit that Amir's [his
son] image emerges before my eyes, and then an occasional
tear flows.

I know how hard this will be for him, because I know
how much he loves me. I especially ask you, Minka, that you
try to console him if you manage to get in touch.

Time is passing with dismal slowness, and I can hardly
wait for the day when I will be with you again. And you will
be sufficient for me for the whole of another world. I would
be happiest of all if we could go together so far away, where
there is nobody else.

Dear Minka, I am terribly worried about Sejdo, Naso,
Biho, and the others. I have heard some very terrible things,
so please let me know what happened to them. Mustafa S.
brought me cigarettes, underwear and the essentials. Thank
him for eternity.

If it hadn't been for that, I would have thought I was
completely alone in the world. I keep wondering where are
those good friends now. But so be it. How is my Beno? Does
he ask for his grandfather? I miss him terribly. Today's the
18th day since I was deprived of my freedom. But to me it
seems like a whole eternity.

I don't even know how many times I've been interrogated, and now the investigation is being conducted by a Judge

Zivko Dragosavljevic. I also asked the lawyer Bereta to attend the interrogations, and I beg you also to engage Shefik P. or Emir Kulenovic, whoever wants to. I don't know how much longer they're going to keep me here.

If you can, buy me some cigarettes somewhere, soap, toothpaste, two to three pairs of underpants, and undershirts, a track suit, shaving set and shaving cream. Don't send me any food because I can't eat anyway. If you have any, send me some ground coffee. Tell Amir to stay at Orhan's and if, God willing, all of this settles down, then you go to him. Tell him to just keep studying, and for the 100th time, tell him that Daddy loves him much much more than he loves himself.

I don't even think about myself any more, but he must be an honest and honorable man. It is inconceivable for me all of this that is happening to us. Is life so unpredictable and so brutal? I remember how this time last year we were rejoicing over building a house, and now see where we are. I feel as if I'd never been alive.

I try to fight it by remembering everything that was beautiful with you and the children and all those I love. That's all for this time, because I don't have any strength any more.

Give my greetings to all who ask about me, and to you and the children I love very, very much.

Muhamed

Treachery on a Mountain Road

Serb Soldiers Rob, Rape and Terrify Thousands
of Fleeing Muslims

Vlasic Mountain, Bosnia-Herzegovina, November 20, 1992

The narrow road carved out of the mountainside is strewn with suitcases, toys and clothing piled several feet high, the remnants of a nation in flight. Corpses often litter the ravine below. There is no guardrail for most of the cliffside path—indeed, no protection of any kind. Down this treacherous serpentine, Bosnia's Serb military has herded about 40,000 Muslim and Croat civilians over the past four months, chasing them at gunpoint into the still free portions of central Bosnia.

Every 30 feet or so along the two-mile gauntlet, Serb soldiers cluster in groups of five or six, fire their submachine guns in the air and brandish knives as they rob and rape the terrified expellees, according to witnesses. In the melees, usually in darkness, the men, women and children often abandon everything, even their identity papers.

"They robbed the people, they took their gold, their money, their jewelry, everything of value. They stripped the clothes off the men. I was naked as a newborn baby," said Skija, 36, from Kotor Vares, who made it down the mountain on October 17.

Skija, who asked to be identified only by his nickname, said he witnessed Serb guards murder two men and then toss them into the ravine. Local authorities in nearby Travnik said at least 40 refugees had been killed in this way. Doctors at Travnik's hospital confirmed the two deaths and said they had admitted another man with severe knife wounds. A woman gave birth in the no-man's-land during the October 17 convoy.

"The people causing problems on the road were beyond anyone's control," said Beat Schweitzer, the chief Red Cross delegate in Banja Luka, who accompanied the convoy to Travnik. It was the first convoy to be monitored by the International Red Cross.

Muslims and Croats fleeing ethnic cleansing in northern Bosnia describe the trek down Vlasic Mountain as the terror to end all terrors, yet they believe it also represents their last hope for survival. Since Bosnia's immediate neighbor, Croatia, closed its borders because other countries have refused to share the burden of refugees, it has been the sole path of escape.

Bosnian Serb leader Radovan Karadzic could not be reached for comment last night, but in the past he has denied all allegations of massacres, rape, or even detention of Muslim and Croat civilians by Serb forces trying to expel them from territories they claim for themselves. A Serb military commander atop Vlasic Mountain, who refused to give his name, told *Newsday*: "Everything we do up here is to ensure security. We deal with people in the most humanitarian way."

Bosnian officials in Travnik said that about 40,000 refugees had made it down the mountain. There are many reports of mass graves north of Vlasic Mountain, where buses full of military-age men have been diverted and the passengers reportedly slaughtered.

Several times a week, a slight, intense man, Zvonko Bajo, drives up Vlasic Mountain. Bajo, a Croat, heads the commission on war prisoner exchanges for Travnik and is usually the first city official to greet the expellees, who often arrive barefoot, unannounced and under fire. He also goes to talk with the Bosnian Serb military officials who control the refugee flow.

Last week, after organizing the first purely civilian

exchange since the war began in April, Bajo obtained permission from the Serb side for a *Newsday* reporter and photographer to join him at the top. He hung a flag with a red cross made by his wife from a small tree branch out the window of his modest green sedan.

A short time earlier, at a preliminary encounter on the plateau at 6,500 feet, Bajo said, the Serbs threatened his life, claiming he had not brought all the Serbs they had placed on a list. They failed to deliver everybody they promised, Bogdan Ristic, Bajo's Serb counterpart, told *Newsday*. A partial exchange took place, and on the descent, the Serbs began shooting at targets in the valley. Bajo drove down the mountain with lights out. "It often happens," he said.

An eerie silence hovered over the plateau. This is the place where refugees disembark with a few belongings from the beat-up and sometimes shot-up buses in the Serb government-organized convoys from elsewhere in northern Bosnia. Usually they have been robbed and assaulted repeatedly en route. Refugees say the plateau is the staging point for the final nightmare, the walk down the serpentine.

The only building, a ski lodge, had been gutted by fire, and Serb officers, operating out of a small trailer, quickly spotted their first Western journalist visitors. "Tell your readers that Serbs want a civilized world," said a short-cropped, gray-haired officer who refused to identify himself. He spoke in Serbo-Croatian and harangued the American reporter for insufficient fluency in the language.

As he spoke about the humanitarian treatment of refugees passing through his territory, half a dozen men in khaki uniforms without insignia silently approached across a grassy knoll. They did not utter a word, but surrounded the visitors, their sheathed knives evident in the dim light of the late afternoon. These, Bajo later confirmed, were the "vultures" who "rob, rape and kill" the refugees fleeing to safety. "They strip them of their clothes. They stab them. They throw them over the cliff," Bajo said. But on this occasion, taking their cue from the Serb officers, they merely stood and watched as the conversation terminated.

A Croat shepherd who tends his flock along the road where the refugees trek said he sometimes hears old people crying out after being thrown down the mountainside. "I've seen parents arrive with dead children in their arms. I've seen some old people arrive in wheelbarrows," he said. "In the last convoy they grabbed leather jackets. If anyone complained, they stabbed him," said the shepherd, who asked that his name not be published.

During one convoy from the town of Kljuc, a group of Croats had been held at the top all night. "The women arrived in tears. They had been taken off the buses and stripped naked. The pretty ones had been taken away. No one could see where they went. They could only hear the screams," said the shepherd.

Treatment varies. On November 3, civilians in an 11-bus convoy from near Kotor Vares were robbed but, according to one female passenger, left unmolested. "They robbed us as we got off the buses. If they saw a leather jacket, they would take it. They went through all our luggage," said the woman, 24, who asked to be identified by the nickname Biba. Biba, who is childless, carried a 3-year-old in a sack on her back, as did other young women in a ruse to avoid being molested.

"Get along, so that your people can kill you," she recalled the Serb soldiers commanding at the top of the trail. Farther down they demanded all their valuables and threatened to kill them, she said. "Because I had no money, they forced me to take off my gold wedding ring." Biba witnessed one assault, when a Serb guard pushed the group leader, a 45-year-old man, down the cliff, but he managed to save himself after dropping 50 feet.

The terror tactics of "ethnic cleansing" that drive Bosnians to risk the dangers of Vlasic Mountain have been widely reported. Less well known are the bureaucratic hurdles Serb authorities make them cross before allowing them to leave.

"In Banja Luka now you need to obtain 12 different certificates to get out of the city. You have to sign away your property to the state. You even have to obtain a certification from the library that you have no overdue books," said Saed Saric, head of the Bosnian Muslim office in Travnik that is collecting data on war crimes. The authorities then collect up to $200 for transportation to the plateau atop Vlasic Mountain, where the expellees are often left for hours aboard buses and robbed at gunpoint.

Skija, whose convoy carried 1,800 people, said he was on one of four buses full of men that were diverted by paramilitaries en route from Kotor Vares with the apparent intention of slaughtering them. After the buses traveled several miles, Bosnian Serb police rescued the men and let the convoy continue. "There was a confrontation, and the local Chetniks opened fire on one of the buses," he said, referring to the World War II Serb royalist force after which many paramilitaries style themselves. Reunited, the convoy's travelers spent the night on Babanovca Mountain, once famous as the site of the European Cup ski jump competition. During the night the Serb guards permitted local paramilitary forces to enter the buses and rob the passengers.

"They took everything they could. On some buses they collected 5,000 or 6,000 marks [$3,000 to $3,500]," Skija said. At 8 A.M. they arrived at the plateau atop Vlasic Mountain and began the walk down. "The bandits were waiting for us. They robbed us again. They demanded our suitcases. They took our jackets. They took our shoes and socks. Fortunately it was warm that day," he said.

Skija, who was interviewed at the offices in Zenica of the Bosnian State Commission on War Crimes, said the first execution he witnessed was of a man about 60 years of age. "He had no money on him, so the Chetnik pulled the trigger and fired 15 to 20 bullets," he said. The soldier stabbed a second man, of roughly the same age, apparently for failing to heed an order to line up along the sheer cliff to be robbed, Skija said.

The expellees proceeded across the Bosnian lines, but several men who had been among the Croat fighters near Kotor Vares exacted rough justice for what they had just witnessed.

"They went back, unarmed, and threw the Chetnik off the cliff," Skija said.

Utterly Neutral

"Probably We Are Too Late.
I Think Everybody Is Too Late."

Travnik, Bosnia-Herzegovina, November 22, 1992

As Serb artillery shells crashed past the minarets into the center of this historic city recently, British UN troops nearby winced as they described their orders, which are to do nothing beyond guarding convoys of humanitarian aid.

With their vastly superior force, the Bosnian Serbs are well placed to capture and destroy this architectural jewel of a city, the gateway to central Bosnia and home to 40,000 residents and expellees. British intelligence reports suggest that the Serbs, who stepped up the attack on Travnik last week, are "going for broke" in Bosnia before President-elect Bill Clinton takes office and considers a policy shift.

The 880-man British battalion group has just completed its deployment in Vitez, just 10 miles south of here. But its mission, laid out by the UN Security Council, is to protect trucks, not people. Should the Serbs seize Travnik and move on to capture Vitez and head toward Sarajevo, taking control of the main supply route from the Adriatic coast to the Bosnian interior, the battlefront would pass right over them.

"We are utterly neutral," said Capt. Lee Smart, a British spokesman at the new UN protection force base in Vitez. "Should the fighting come past us, under the orders we have been given so far, we can't fight anyone." The exception is self-defense. "Should we be attacked, we can defend ourselves," Smart said.

For foreign relief agencies the deployment of the British and other forces under UN control is another case of inadequate humanitarian "Band-aids" that have no impact on the war itself. They say Bosnia could well freeze and starve despite the logistical support provided by Western troops.

"Probably we are too late," said Yves Mauron, the International Red Cross representative in nearby Zenica. "I think everybody is too late. This is the characteristic of this war."

A mood of fatalism pervades Travnik, located in a narrow valley and indefensible from attack by the Serbs who have taken the high ground. Turkish viziers ruled Bosnia from this town from 1699 to 1851, and Nobel Prize–winning author Ivo Andric was born here. But its days as a predominantly Muslim city may be numbered. Because of a split between the ill-armed Muslim forces, who are fighting to preserve a unified Bosnian state, and the better equipped Roman Catholic Croats, who favor partition, the powerful army of the Christian Orthodox Serbs advanced last week to the edge of Turbe, a suburb four miles to the north.

In an interview earlier this month at his front-line headquarters in Turbe, the local Muslim commander expressed only forlorn hope. "The Serbs have tanks and artillery. We are fighting with hunting rifles. All we have is our hands and our hearts," said Reko Sulejman. For months, he said, the Croat forces had refused to deliver military supplies, and the only way for the Muslims to obtain any weapons was through private purchase. For weeks, according to a British intelligence assessment, the Croats took no part in the fighting.

In recent days, the Croats shifted their stance, sending reinforcements to Turbe and setting up a roadblock at the southern end of the narrow valley to prevent fighters from fleeing. But foreign observers say tension between Muslims and Croats is just below the surface and could erupt again.

In the last month, Bosnian Croats attacked Muslims in nearby Novi Travnik in a battle in which 20 died and the entire commercial district and several apartment buildings were destroyed. In Prozor, a predominantly Croat town to the west, the Croat forces sent in tanks and destroyed the Muslim business district. Extreme Croat nationalists have renamed the military police headquarters there the "House of the Ustasha," referring to the World War II force allied with the Nazis. As fighting raged between the Croats and Muslims, the Serbs capitalized on it by seizing the stronghold of Jajce, northwest of Travnik, forcing 45,000 people to flee.

Foreign relief officials say they believe the Croats may have decided to reinforce their position in Travnik, whose population is 45 percent Muslim and 37 percent Croat, with the aim, if the Serbs allow, of later taking control and expelling the Muslim population.

Ivan Sarci, a spokesman for the Bosnian Croat army, disputed any such intent. "Muslims and Croats are defending Travnik together," he said. "There has been no conflict here. We will defend the city as best we know how."

In Travnik the tension is palpable. "This is a city where the Croat officials are reporting to Boban, and the Muslims are reporting to Sarajevo," said Davor Schopf, a local Croat journalist. He referred to Mate Boban, the head of the self-declared autonomous Bosnian Croat state. "The only way it continues to function is because the officials know each other from childhood and try to arrange practical solutions."

Travnik is not only a key northern outpost of the besieged Bosnian government and a gateway to Sarajevo, 55 miles southeast, but it is also the first safe haven for Muslims and Croats fleeing the terror tactics of Serb "ethnic cleansing" aimed at driving the other groups from northern Bosnia.

About 18,000 refugees who survived assaults and robbery by Serb irregulars as they walked down the treacherous Vlasic Mountain fill the schools, sports halls, kindergartens, army barracks and private homes of Travnik. But now Travnik, whose own population is about the same size, is also destitute.

"We have used up all our stocks, our money, our gasoline, our food, our communal reserves," said Mustafa Hockic, a

Muslim member of the city government. "Now our own citizens have been reduced to the state of refugees. Our doctors, our teachers have to go to the public kitchens for food. We now have to organize aid for our own inhabitants."

If Serbs capture Turbe, even the treacherous path down Vlasic Mountain could be closed. And in the Banja Luka region, where the "ethnic cleansing" is proceeding full speed ahead, foreign relief officials said they had no way of guessing how people could escape. Neighboring Croatia and most of Europe have closed their borders to Bosnian refugees.

During daytime lulls in the fighting, children play war in a cemetery overlooking the city. At night horse-drawn carts go back and forth to nearby villages as peasants gather their belongings and flee before the expected Serb advance.

Travnik has no heat. The official reason is that Serb artillery damaged the central heating plant and there is no coal. But in fact, sources said, the city has not started up its central heating plant to avoid offering another target for the Serbs. If the heating plant is destroyed, the city will become virtually uninhabitable in the coming winter.

But the British detachment has its hands tied. "Our mandate is to protect the UN food convoys and to go wherever they want us. Beyond that we're not in a position to get involved," Smart said.

About the only hope for saving the city appears to be quick action by the UN Security Council on an Austrian proposal to use military force to establish safe zones in Travnik and four other Bosnian cities—Sarajevo, Gorazde, Tuzla and Bihac. Austria's plan, modeled on the safe havens created by the United States and Britain for Iraqi Kurds after the Gulf war, is intended to stem the flood of refugees expected this winter if the Serbs continue their conquest of Bosnia.

It would require a far greater military force than the 20,000 UN troops now deployed in Bosnia, and, an Austrian official acknowledged, would amount to an intervention through the back door.

"We are convinced that if limited military action had been taken one year ago, this war would never have occurred," said the official, who spoke on condition of anonymity. "We are also convinced that we will all be dragged in later, with far higher casualties, far higher human costs and far more destruction."

The official said that the United States, which has no troops in Bosnia, seems in favor of the plan and that France, with 4,000 troops in Bosnia, has given tentative support, but that Britain has expressed strong reservations because it might put its 2,600 troops at risk.

A senior official at the UN High Commission on Refugees said the idea of a safe zone was "very appealing" but that to implement it would require a major military commitment that he doubted world leaders would make. The official, who asked not to be named, said such an approach would also be "another humanitarian solution for something that is not humanitarian. It is another case of dealing with consequences, not causes. Don't look for humanitarian solutions. Look for real solutions," he said.

❖

Course Proves Deadly

Muslim Villagers Defy Serbs, but Few Survive Trek

Travnik, Bosnia-Herzegovina, November 27, 1992

After a long trek through the rugged wilderness, the legendary fighters of Vecici straggled into this besieged Bosnian town on November 9 and counted their losses. Their column had set off one week earlier from the Muslim village in north Bosnia with more than 600 people, but only 115 made it through. For five months they had fought the Serbs from the trenches around their village near Kotor Vares, part of a home guard defense they said had once stretched 25 miles along the Vrbanja River Valley. "We had created such problems for them," said the fighters' 28-year-old commander, "but we were one spot in the whole sea."

Depleted in their supplies, deserted by their Croat allies and facing a Serb ultimatum to surrender or watch the village be destroyed, they chose the course of defiance. They decided to try to escape with their weapons to Bosnian government–held territory, using the back supply route across mountains, ravines and forests they thought had been their secret.

But at three points along the 60-mile route, the Serbs set up ambushes. And while the fighters were moving, Serbs conquered the government territory they had hoped to reach, near Jajce. When they finally reached Travnik, they calculated that up to 400 people—300 fighters and most of the 100 women and children—had been killed or captured or were missing. The International Red Cross said it has been able to trace only about 100 survivors.

"We had to walk over dead bodies. We had to leave the

wounded behind," said the commander, who for reasons of his own safety asked to be identified only by his nickname, Aga. "We knew there was no way out if we remained there. It was very hard to make the decision, but we had to leave the dead behind."

The fighters of Vecici typify the tragedy of the Bosnian Muslim resistance—destitute and hungry but willing to fight on, although they are not sure for what. "When you see the way the world reacts, you begin to think maybe the world wants you to be annihilated," Aga said. "Why don't they lift the [arms] embargo? We were fighting with rifles against tanks. If we'd had one-tenth of what the Serbs had, we could have stayed."

Vecici, with a population of only 1,150, became the last major armed holdout in north Bosnia by the geographical quirk that it is located in a canyon that protects it from aerial bombardment. The Bosnian Serb army used its formidable arsenal against the village. "They would shoot individuals with tanks, even our livestock," recalled Zuhdija Becula, 19, another of the Vecici fighters who made it to Travnik. Fighters say that at least 85 townspeople were killed in the attacks but that the Vecici fighters exacted as many as 500 casualties when the Serbs twice sent infantry against the village.

But in October, Serbia and Croatia began reaching agreements to ease the confrontation between them, and several Croat villages that had fought alongside Vecici laid down their arms. Escorted by the International Red Cross, the Croat fighters journeyed to Travnik down the treacherous Mount Vlasic trail, where they were assaulted and robbed, and at least two people were killed. The Vecici men were convinced that as Muslims they would never be able to survive such a convoy. "We knew what was waiting for us. It is better to die in battle than be tortured," Aga said. "We decided that we are fighters, and we would go on our own."

The Red Cross brokered a deal on October 28 under which the Serbs agreed to transport the women and children of Vecici to Travnik. Other than being robbed of their valuables, all made it safely, refugees said.

The fighters set out on November 2 after slaughtering their livestock for food and using the remaining flour to bake bread. The trip was doomed from the start. Some sisters, wives and children—118 people altogether—insisted on accompanying the 500 fighters. "This hampered our movements and fighting abilities," Aga said. The women feared they would be raped if they went by convoy, as had happened before. "In August," Aga said, "not one of the girls between 14 and 30 got here without being raped."

The enormous column stumbled into its first ambush during the first night at a wood between Vecici and the town of Skender Vakuf. One person was killed, "but the women and children panicked," Aga said. The group split into two parts, and the second group lost its way. Most were subsequently captured.

Having been exposed, Aga's lead group began traveling by day, and on the second day they stumbled into the second trap, a minefield laid by the Serbs in a narrow gorge of the Grabovica River. Five of the Vecici scouts were injured in an explosion; four killed themselves on the spot, but the fifth begged to be rescued, Aga recounted. The group picked him up and was proceeding along the river gorge when "all hell broke loose."

"The Serbs were on top shooting down at us with a machine gun. The situation was hopeless. All around you could see people wounded and dying," Aga recalled.

In desperation, the fighters divided and went down both sides of the canyon straight into the path of the Serbs for about a half-mile, he said. "We started shooting back and managed to break them up and throw them back," he said. That was where they had to abandon the dead and the wounded, with some of the fighters staying behind to care for the wounded. Only about 90 to 100 of the 300 Aga was leading, including three women, were able to continue.

At nightfall they moved toward Skender Vakuf. While

crossing a main road, they stumbled into the third ambush. "All of a sudden, the Chetniks started firing from across the road," said Aga, referring to the bearded World War II royalists after whom many Serb soldiers style themselves. "They were hidden in a trench. I threw myself down on the road. Then all hell broke loose. It started to rain. In the bedlam we all scattered. We couldn't find each other. We couldn't call out."

Most of the group climbed down to a swollen stream and walked down its middle to avoid mines. "We were in water up to our necks because of the rain. The whole time they were shooting at us. It was a nightmare," said Refik Pasic, 27, another fighter.

Thirty men did not make it. Some had been caught, some killed. The group was down to 69 men and three women. At dawn they gathered and moved toward what they thought was Bosnian territory. But unbeknownst to them, the town of Jajce had fallen to the Serbs, and there were no Bosnian forces in the area.

"We thought we were in free territory. But livestock was wandering around," Pasic said. They got directions from civilians and eventually caught up with Bosnian troops then in retreat. "We were all very tired. I have no idea how far we traveled. We had gone days without food," Pasic added. They found 19 men from their group who had gone astray, and 91 walked into Travnik together, cold and wet.

"The one thing I was most frightened of was being injured. I knew I would have to kill myself," said Aga.

The story of the other 300 from Vecici was a catastrophe. Three men who were in that group said the entire 300 had been captured in the village of Grabovica. "We surrendered without a fight. They let the women and children go. But they tortured the men and killed them," said Becula.

According to Muhamed Zec, 65, the Serbs took about 40 men to the post office in nearby Skender Vakuf and put them into basement rooms that "were cold enough to keep ice cream." There "they started to kick us and beat us with truncheons and brass knuckles." "There was blood running down the walls from the beatings. They'd bang your head against the wall. They beat you with a cane," recalled Djeval Kovacic, 30. "I saw one man who had wounds, and they put salt on them."

The three were among 20 who were later sent to Manjaca, an army-run, so-called prisoner-of-war camp, and then taken to Mount Vlasic and released to a Travnik city official on November 11. Four women were brought over the mountain separately.

Seval, 25, a fighter in Aga's group who asked that his last name not be used, said he had met in the woods a Vecici fighter from the other group who said he had escaped a massacre in which 150 men from his group had been executed in groups of 10. There was no independent confirmation of that account.

Glas, the official daily in the Bosnian Serb capital of Banja Luka, reported that about 300 combatants from Vecici had used women and children as shields in their escape attempt and that the "valiant" Serb military had "dealt with" 100 to 200 of them, and another 100 had surrendered. An official of the Red Cross in Banja Luka said he had located about 100 Vecici fighters who were either being detained or treated in the hospital.

Today the fighters of Vecici are stuck in Travnik, a town under bombardment by the Serbs, where a typhus epidemic has broken out among the 18,000 other refugees.

"Winter is coming. We have no clothes, only what we are wearing. The Serbs have stolen everything. We had been quite well off. Here we are beggars. We stand in line for food," Aga said.

They would return to battle, Aga said. "We were fighting as guerrillas against tanks, against aircraft. If the world helped us now, we would come back to zero. We've lost our family life, our jobs, our cars, our houses. But we'd still go back."

The fighters believe they acted in self-defense. "No one of good will could want this. No ordinary man," Aga said. "You can only imagine if this happened to your family. How would you act?"

❖

Nowhere Men

Hundreds of Civilians Languish in Limbo of Serb Detention Camp

Batkovic, Bosnia-Herzegovina, January 24, 1993

In the dark void of the vast sheds, pigeons fly between their perches in the rafters while on the concrete floor below, the sound of coughing men punctuates the chill air. Here in two hangars where grain was once stored, hundreds of Bosnian Muslim and Croat detainees, survivors of Bosnian Serb death camps, huddle together or lie under layers of blankets on their lice-infested straw mattresses.

There is neither heat nor electric light, and between Christmas and New Year's Day the temperature inside the sheds dropped to about zero. Water canteens froze under the detainees' pillows, and their blankets "practically stood up on end," a Red Cross official said. Now the temperature hovers just above freezing.

"We couldn't sleep because it was so cold," said Kemal Sobani, 23. One elderly man died, and in their frozen stupor, detainees, as well as wardens, left him there for two days.

In the outdoor latrines, which consist of planks placed over a ditch, ice formed on the boards, and more than a few men slipped into the pit of human waste.

The men had the misfortune of living in Muslim or Croat villages conquered by Bosnian Serbs in their quest to create a greater Serbia on the ruins of multiethnic Yugoslavia. They are still being held, five months after Bosnian Serb leader Radovan Karadzic promised under world pressure to release all civilian detainees unilaterally. According to the camp officials, those remaining must await a prisoner exchange. Despite the lofty rhetoric of Western politicians and prominent figures who visited them since *Newsday* disclosed the existence of death camps last August, the men say they have no idea when they will get out.

The 970 men here range in age from 18 to over 60. Some are veterans of four camps in the past eight months, and three Croats held here were arrested by Serbs 15 months ago, during a different war. All are civilians. Witnesses to the murder and torture of thousands of fellow Muslims and Croats, they still have no idea why they are being held.

The last group arrived in mid-December, living proof of what they, at least, view as another broken promise. They had been held for months at Manjaca, a bigger camp more than 100 miles west. But after a visit to Manjaca on November 28 by Elie Wiesel, who won the Nobel Peace Prize for his writings on surviving the Nazi Holocaust, they thought they were headed for freedom.

"Elie Wiesel promised us we would all be free," said one prisoner, 31-year-old Refik Bosnic. "I will do everything I can to get you out of here," he quoted Wiesel as saying. Manjaca was closed December 13 and several thousand prisoners freed, but that was the start of a human shell game for Bosnic and 500 others.

According to Lt. Col. Petar Dmitrovic, in charge of the camp here, 532 Manjaca detainees were brought to Batkovic; 130 of them were taken to Sarajevo and freed in an exchange, while 401 stayed at Batkovic. The Red Cross has been unable to confirm the release of the 130 and lists them as disappeared.

Those who met Wiesel may even have been singled out for extended detention. Of the 10 men who briefed him at Manjaca, among them Bosnic, nine are still detained, Bosnic said. Wiesel could not be reached for comment Friday or yesterday.

The Geneva-based International Red Cross regularly

delivers food, clothes and cigarettes, but its staff was unable until this week to find stoves that will provide even a modicum of heat in spaces that in reality cannot be adequately heated. And they have done little to improve the sanitary facilities. The detainees can use faucets outdoors and wash in the trough below when the weather permits, but Bosnic said he had gone four months without a bath.

But some things have improved, according to prisoners who have been here since May. After protests by Serb villagers, authorities replaced the guards who beat the prisoners.

According to data they have given to the Red Cross, Bosnia's Serbs are detaining 1,300 Muslims and Croats; Muslim forces currently hold 900 Serbs; and Croat forces hold 530 Serbian civilians in conditions comparable to those at Batkovic. Those are the official figures, but the U.S. State Department believes as many as 70,000 civilians are still being held in Bosnia, mainly by Serbs. The Red Cross cannot substantiate the figure, but admits it has been unable to visit one of the most notorious Serb prisons, in the town of Foca.

Bosnic, a salesman and cafe owner, said he was arrested along with 41 others in his hometown of Bosanska Dubica last June 25. "They took all the people who owned businesses. None of us were even asked about the war. None of us had any weapons. They told us we'd be freed in ten to fourteen days." He stayed in Manjaca almost six months, then was transferred to Batkovic.

Zlata Jakupovic, 19, was arrested in the town of Kozarac in early May. Batkovic is his fourth camp. First he was taken to Kereterm, outside Prijedor, where he said he was beaten daily. Then he went to Omarska, where U.S. government interviewers believe as many as 5,000 men were slaughtered. Omarska was closed at the beginning of August, and he was taken to Manjaca. There, he said, he waited with other prisoners in buses before the camp gates and saw guards kill eight men by slitting their throats. "They were all very rich, and the guards wanted to know where they had their money."

Jakupovic celebrated his nineteenth birthday at Manjaca and was transferred here December 13. When he was asked whether he heard from his family, his eyes filled with tears. "I don't know if anyone is alive. I have not gotten a letter," he said. Kozarac was leveled by the Serb-run Bosnian army in July, and its 30,000 residents were massacred, deported or sent to concentration camps.

Josica Cendric, a 31-year-old car mechanic from the Croatian town of Slunj, was arrested by the Serb army on November 18, 1991, along with two other Croats, while riding a bus from Cazin to Zagreb. They were taken to a Serb prison at Stara Gradiska, and then early last June to Manjaca. "We weren't soldiers. There were never any charges against us," he said.

Across the shed from Cendric, Alija Drljacic, 62, lay under a stack of blankets. Serb authorities held him and 700 others at Bosanski Samac from early last summer until they closed the camp on December 27, when they transferred him to Batkovic. Like others, he swears he never carried a weapon and made no attempt to fight the conquering Serb forces.

The Samac detainees said they are not yet ready to describe the atrocities they witnessed. "We'll talk about it when we get out," said Amis Bihic, 19.

Dmitrovic admitted that all the detainees at his camp are civilians. "We do not have prisoners of war," he said. So why have they been taken into custody and held here in defiance of the Geneva conventions on war, which prohibit the arbitrary detention of civilians? According to Dmitrovic, their towns and villages happened to be in a war corridor. "Many fought as civilians," he asserted, "and were arrested." Meanwhile, their houses "have been destroyed in the fighting, and they have nowhere to go."

Five months after this article appeared, most of the prisoners were still at Batkovic. As of mid-June, International Red Cross figures showed that the Serbs still held 1,023 civilians, 809 of them at Batkovic; the Bosnian government held 993, and Bosnian Croats, 400. Although the U.S. government early in 1993 had estimated that there were as many as 70,000 detainees, Red Cross sources said they could not verify this figure. At the same time, the Red Cross had not obtained access to several known detention camps at Serb-conquered towns on the Drina River, and thousands of persons remained unaccounted for.

Villagers Ease Pain in Camps

Batkovic, Bosnia-Herzegovina, January 24, 1993

All last summer, buses and trucks packed with Muslim and Croat prisoners trundled down the narrow farm road past Ilija Gajic's vegetable farm. The army never consulted the villagers when it set up the camp in the state grain-storage sheds. Gajic feared that the worst of Balkan history was repeating itself.

"Concentration camps never bring anything for anyone," said the 62-year-old Serb who presides over the assembly in this village of 4,000. "I felt bad watching this happening."

As reports emerged of beatings and deaths, he and other leaders of the village decided to protest. His is one of the untold stories in this war of unremitting cruelty—the story of Serbs who took a risk to improve conditions for their fellow citizens.

"We wanted to make a goodwill gesture. We wanted them to be treated as we would wish the other side to treat our prisoners," he said.

Early in September, Gajic led a delegation to the nearby army headquarters in Bijelina and demanded that guards who had been beating prisoners be replaced. "They were not from around here. They had had victims in their families and wanted to exact revenge," Gajic said. "So we asked the authorities to put in local people."

The military command at first refused even to say who was in charge of the camp, he recalled. The tone of the discussion sharpened. One of the delegation told the military commanders, "We don't want a Jasenovac," a reference to the concentration camp set up by Croatian fascists during

World War II, where tens of thousands of Serbs, Jews and Gypsies were put to death.

"Any good man would say that," said Gajic. "We didn't want to let the village be blamed for whatever happened. We wanted to save the reputation of the village."

In the presence of guards, prisoners are still reluctant to talk about the cruelty of the earlier period. But they confirmed the stories told by released detainees of beatings with two-by-fours, rampant dysentery fed by terrible sanitary conditions, and elaborate ruses devised to fool visiting delegations into thinking there was no one under 18 or over 60 in the camp.

According to detainees, at least 20 had died of beatings or maltreatment up to September, but conditions improved significantly after the intervention of the villagers.

The conditions remain primitive, but several hundred detainees now go to work six days a week in a nearby factory, where they have better meals, although no pay. The detainees compliment the guards, and the guards welcome the praise. "We feel we don't have to beat the prisoners," said Dragolic, one of the new local guards. "We talk to them." There is now even a television set in each of the sheds, and over the New Year, the guards brought the detainees bottles of slivovitz, a plum brandy.

"I think Serbs are not so bad as everyone wants to make them out to be," Gajic said. "There are probably other examples of that, not only in Batkovic."

❖

"One by One"

The Ordeal of Women Raped and Beaten in Bosnia Camp

Zagreb, Croatia, February 21, 1993

In the gulag of Serb detention camps in Bosnia, Omarska was synonymous with massive atrocities. As many as 4,000 Muslim and Croatian men died there of beatings, torture or disease, witnesses say. Several were castrated before fellow detainees, others forced at gunpoint to have oral sex with each other.

Women were held at Omarska, too. The 33 female captives at Omarska suffered a horrendous ordeal—rapes, beatings and perhaps even worse, according to testimony obtained by *Newsday*. When the iron mine-turned-concentration camp was closed in August following eyewitness accounts in *Newsday* on abuses in the Serb camps, 29 of the women were released, according to a former detainee.

In the same rooms where the men were interrogated and beaten by day, women allegedly were molested by night. "The first thing we had to do each evening was clean up the blood and the mess of those who had been tortured during the day," recalled Jadranka Cigelj, 45, an ethnic Croat from the north Bosnian city of Prijedor. Cigelj, a lawyer and political activist, said she was held in Omarska for seven weeks, from June 14 to Aug. 3.

"They took the women one by one," she said, describing the nightly beatings and rapes. "Not every one every day. They had a timetable. I was taken out four nights. Every night, a different one." She alleged that one of the men who raped her was Zeljko Mejahic, the commander of the guards at the camp.

Cigelj's account was corroborated by Western diplomats with access to accounts by other women who had been held at Omarska. Cigelj, who has become a leading activist in a growing effort to document alleged war crimes in Bosnia, told *Newsday* that 11 of the women who had been held at Omarska are now in Zagreb and are prepared to testify that they were raped.

"It is beyond the shadow of a doubt" that women were raped at Omarska, said a Western diplomat, who asked not to be identified by name or country. The same diplomat estimated on the basis of witness statements that as many as 4,000 men were killed at Omarska.

Mejahic denied there had been any rapes at the camp, which he described as "an investigative center." He said in a written statement that only Cigelj and eight other women had been in Omarska and that they had been held there for no more than a day or two. He contemptuously rejected Cigelj's rape accusation, saying he would not "lean a bicycle" on her, no less rape her.

"The women were treated correctly, and all the policemen had instructions to keep their distance from them," Mejahic said in the statement transmitted to *Newsday* by Lt. Col. Milovan Milutinovic, spokesman for the Bosnian Serb army in Banja Luka.

"In all responsibility I can state that there was no attempt at rape, and even less that I raped Jadranka Cigelj. I don't know why I would do that, because she is 45 years old, while I am 26, and I don't need a woman as old as that, particularly as she is a bad and unattractive woman. The way she was, I wouldn't lean a bicycle on her, let alone rape her. These are just lies," Mejahic said.

Cigelj described Mejahic as a killer, an allegation U.S. government interviewers said they heard repeatedly during debriefings in the fall with recently released Omarska detainees. "He ordered killings. He himself killed prisoners," Cigelj said.

Mejahic, interviewed by *Newsday* in September, said only two men died at Omarska, both of natural causes.

Reports in *Newsday* and other publications that the conquering Serb forces engaged in systematic rape of Muslim and Croat women and minors prompted a flurry of investigations by international committees. A probe authorized by the European Community came to the conclusion that at least 20,000 Muslim women had been raped during the Serb conquest. Some of the rapes occurred in special detention centers set up for women and children.

Omarska, a death camp where men were tortured, killed or starved, fell into a different category, for women were held there apparently to do the dishes and the cleanup at the facility's cafeteria.

Cigelj said that, from a count of the dishes used during lunch—the one meal each day that the men had to wolf down in one or two minutes—the Serbs had held more than 2,700 men at Omarska on the average—10 times the number Mejahic had acknowledged during the interview with a *Newsday* reporter at the camp site in September.

Cigelj was arrested and taken to Omarska on June 14, along with eight other women active in politics or local government in Prijedor. "I was doing the cleaning in my apartment when two armed police officers with automatic weapons, grenades and bayonets came for me," she told *Newsday*.

In the interview and in a signed statement on file at the Croatian information center where she now works, she described the beatings she endured and gave a graphic account of how Silvije Saric, the president of the Prijedor county committee of the Croatian Democratic Union, was beaten to death in front of her eyes.

Newsday already has reported the disappearance and death at Omarska of Muhamed Cehajic, the Slav Muslim mayor of the nearby town of Prijedor, and other top Prijedor politicians, professional people and businessmen. Cigelj was the union's vice president.

At the Prijedor police station, she spent an entire day in a small room that was "sprinkled with the blood of those who . . . were probably either beaten or killed," she said. Together with two other women political activists, Edna Dautovic, a Muslim, and Jadranka Pates, a Croat, she was brought to Omarska by police car.

Inside the Omarska administration building, they were joined by six other women, among them the leading attorneys in Prijedor: Mirseta Tivac, a district court judge; Jasminka Hadzibegovic, the deputy district attorney; and Edina Nautovic, another county judge. It was a who's who of women in government and the professions. There were altogether four teachers, three lawyers in addition to Cigelj, two economists, two women with college degrees in economics, two doctors, one dentist, one electrical engineer, one metallurgical engineer, one nurse and the rest high school graduates. All were Muslims except three Croats, Cigelj said.

They spent the next day in the mine complex's cafeteria, then returned to the room where they were to sleep. "The room did not look the same as we had left it. It was all smeared with blood. Even the walls were sprinkled with blood, and broken clubs were lying on the table. These were special clubs made of boiled beechwood, and they were used to beat people until . . . [the clubs] were reduced to splinters," she said.

That night guards beat her "with a club all over my back." All during the night, they alternated beatings, first Saric, and then her. "They beat me with rifle butt ends on my back. I still bear the consequences—broken ribs and a deformed thorax." She fainted, and when she came to, was beaten again, Cigelj said.

On the fifth day, she learned the "charge" against her: Her name purportedly had been found on a list of prominent non-Serbs who were to make up a transitional government to replace the mixed government of Muslims, Serbs and Croats in Prijedor county. She said she had never heard about the list before it was shown to her.

The rapes began on July 18. The women slept in two rooms, and at 1:15 A.M., a uniformed man stood in the hallway and called out her name. "The man had a captain's rank. He was wearing army clothes and civilian shoes. Later I found out that he was a local from Omarska, a reserve officer by the name of Nedeljko Grabovac," she said.

"Suddenly the lights went out. He grabbed my hand and dragged me out in the corridor. He pushed me into the bathroom. He hit me over the head with the handle of his revolver and cut my skin, then he took the rifle off his shoulder and started beating me. He started to rape me."

On three successive nights, she said, she was beaten and raped by Mejahic and by guards named Mladen Radic and Kos Miloica. Then it stopped. Besides the mental scars, Cigelj said she bears physical scars as well. She has several broken ribs, which healed without medical attention while she was in the camp, she said, and still has problems walking due to a hip injury. "When I cough, I sometimes throw up blood, because the ribs press my lungs," she said.

By night, they were beaten. By day, they watched and heard guards torture the men. "We could hear the screams. They would torture a man as long as he could bear it. If he was lucky, he would survive," she said. "If he was dumb enough to show that he felt better after a couple of days, they would take him out again. In the mornings, you could see bodies lying in the grass. That is how we knew who was missing."

Until the last days of the camp, the women had the kitchen patrol. "We were intellectuals, and they needed women to work in the kitchens. They thought they would humiliate us."

Then on August 3, the camp closed. "We were given orders to clean the windows. They stressed that they wanted everything to be spotless." Outside, men were washing down the building wall. "It was stained with human blood and human brains. They were brushing it frantically." The "final psychological torture" came when the camp guards read out a list of 29 women who would be released. Her name was included in that group. Four were not. "They have never been seen again," she said.

❖

Going Nowhere:
UN War Crime Commission Bogged Down in Bosnia Death Camp Probe

Geneva, Switzerland, March 4, 1993

Five months after a reluctant UN Security Council announced a formal probe into reports of death camps, mass rape and deportations in Bosnia, the panel intended to prepare the way for a war crimes tribunal is bogged down in confusion. U.S. diplomats are livid that the so-called Commission of Experts has, in their view, achieved almost nothing since its appointment in October. It hasn't held a hearing or sent a mission into Bosnia, or even requested the news media to provide copies of their stories and videotapes.

Morris Abram, the outgoing U.S. ambassador to the United Nations in Geneva, said the commission hasn't made a serious effort to prepare for war crimes trials. "They meet once in a while," said Abram, who was part of the prosecution staff at the Nuremberg tribunals of Nazi war criminals. "They don't have a staff to amount to anything. They don't have resources, people right now interviewing witnesses, who can tell you about who the camp guards were. . . . If this is serious you've got to have a large number of people involved. And moreover, you've got to start dealing with the problem before the trail gets cold."

The chairman of the UN panel, retired Dutch academic Frits Kalshoven, says he was instructed by "authoritative persons" in the UN not to pursue Serbian politicians such as Slobodan Milosevic, president of Serbia, and Radovan Karadzic, leader of the Bosnian Serbs. Both men were named as potential war criminals by former U.S. Secretary of State Lawrence Eagleburger.

Kalshoven admits serious qualms about convening war crimes trials, and tells visitors he does not know why he got the job. He says he received instructions to limit his probe from the UN Legal Office in New York, which reports to UN Secretary-General Boutros Boutros-Ghali. But the UN deputy legal adviser says he never said any such thing and suggested in an interview that the source of Kalshoven's guidance might be Cyrus Vance and David Owen, UN mediators in the Bosnia crisis.

Ambassador Abram made the same suggestion.

"Go talk with Vance and Owen," he said. Vance acknowledged he had met twice with Kalshoven, but he categorically denied any attempt to influence him not to investigate top officials.

Yet the bottom line is that after five months, the commission assigned to prepare the way for the first war crimes tribunal since Nuremberg has achieved next to nothing, according to a wide range of sources. Its sole report, issued January 26, noted that "grave breaches" of international humanitarian law had been committed but did not say where they had occurred or where the principal responsibility might lie.

Kalshoven has questioned whether war crimes trials should occur within the next decade. "There is no way a tribunal could work in the present atmosphere of anti-Serb propaganda, which is rampant all over the world," he told a western European diplomat late last year. The diplomat, who spoke on condition of anonymity, reported the episode to his government. According to his account, Kalshoven said, "It will never be possible to have an objective procedure. . . . And by the way, a tribunal can take place only at the end of the conflict," he was quoted as saying. He agreed that might be 10 years or more. The Nuremberg trials began in November 1945, months after World War II ended.

And although the Security Council has since approved the tribunal in principle, Kalshoven told *Newsday* last week that it "is quite some while off" and added he was "not overly optimistic" one would ever come about.

Richard Schifter, U.S. ambassador to the UN Human Rights Commission here, said on February 9 that "the horrors of Bosnia are surely among the greatest tragedies to befall humankind in the second half of the twentieth century."

But there are many who think the meager results of the Kalshoven panel are what the nations in the Security Council intended. Council members often have been ambivalent about human rights abuses in the Bosnia crisis. With Britain in the lead, the council has made signing a peace agreement a higher priority than prosecution, many diplomats say. The appointment of the Kalshoven commission, a hesitant first step toward war crimes proceedings, was spurred by news accounts of the atrocities last summer.

"It's not much more than a cosmetic effort," George Kenney said of the UN plans for a tribunal. Kenney resigned as State Department Yugoslavia desk officer last August to protest the Bush administration's passivity in the Bosnia conflict. "Measure it empirically," he said. "How much resources have they put in?"

Indeed, the total budget for the Kalshoven commission, according to Ralph Zacklin, the New York–based UN officer who oversees it, is $690,000 for nine months. This pays salaries and travel costs. U.S. diplomats are scathing about the Kalshoven commission's method of operations. Kalshoven's staff consists of two staff members sent by Zacklin's office and two secretaries. Kalshoven is on salary, but the four commission members are paid a per diem and travel expenses.

"The commission is going nowhere," said a U.S. diplomatic source speaking on condition of anonymity. "It's like asking a quadriplegic to go out and run a race." Said another: "It would be better to cut our losses, go immediately to a tribunal, start up with enough resources, computers, prosecutors and so on, and start over again."

Supported by a tiny staff, the Kalshoven commission consists of five men. Only Kalshoven is paid full time, and only two of the four part-time members have actively participated in operations. Torkel Opsahl, 62, a Norwegian expert on human rights, has been unable to attend most meetings. He told *Newsday* he was appointed "probably because I am very cautious in talking with the press." Keba Mbaye, 69, a retired member of the International Court of Justice from Senegal, also has been unable to attend all meetings.

William Finrick, 50, a law expert in the Canadian military, and the Egyptian-born Cherif Bassiouni, 56, have been the most active. The panel has set up a data bank to collate reports submitted by UN members. Bassiouni accomplished this with the help of volunteers at Chicago's DePaul University and a $200,000 donation from George Soros, a New York–based financier with an interest in human rights causes, to buy computers. This sum is on top of the UN–based budget. The database for the moment consists mainly of reports filed by UN member states, private nongovernmental human rights groups, and the special representative of the UN Human Rights Commission, Tadeusz Mazowiecki. Only 10 countries, among them the United States, France and Germany, but not Britain, have submitted reports.

Kalshoven, 69, has told visitors he is overwhelmed by the job. Zacklin, the deputy legal adviser who closely monitors its activities, said Kalshoven was appointed largely because he was retired and available. Other commission members say Kalshoven, a leading expert in his field who never rose beyond the middle levels in the Dutch civil service, is illsuited to the bureaucratic infighting needed to secure the resources for the commission. His initial report was full of legal jargon and little substance, diplomats said.

"Kalshoven narrowly interpreted his mandate as sorting

alleged acts of criminal activity into categories, those that were truly crimes against humanity from those that fall short of the accepted standard of definition," said J. Kenneth Blackwell, a U.S. delegate to the UN Human Rights Commission here. "But the question of whether or not war crimes have been committed is extremely academic. You have to have Jonathan Swift's imagination to think these don't meet modern-day definitions. In the meantime, where's the apparatus and resources to build the foundation for a tribunal? To be positioned for immediate action, work has to begin now."

But in taking his slow and limited approach, Kalshoven had ample reinforcement. Kalshoven said he was given restrictive instructions at the first meeting with Zacklin and his superior, Undersecretary General for Legal affairs Carl Fleischauer of Germany, in early November. He first revealed the instruction to an American diplomat in mid-January and confirmed it to *Newsday* last week.

"Of course, we, the members of the commission present, discussed our mandate with them, the members of the Legal Office. We had the same interpretation of the resolution," he said. "It does not stand out from that resolution that we would have to look for persons in the first stage, whether they are low or high up. . . . Our resolution simply does not mention persons."

Zacklin denied during two interviews that he or Fleischauer gave such an instruction to Kalshoven. "There has never been any suggestion of separating the leaders from the rest. . . . No one has ever suggested we should white-wash Mr. Karadzic. We just want to establish the facts wherever they fall," he told a *Newsday* reporter in New York.

Some inside the commission view Zacklin as the principal brakeman. A Briton, he was said by one commission member to be "absolutely in line with the British government." Zacklin said he receives his orders from Boutros-Ghali and that it was against UN guidelines to take them from anyone else, including his own government. Yet he defended the narrow guidelines. "The commission had a very limited mandate, to make a report to the secretary-general with its conclusions as to the commission of grave breaches of international humanitarian law. . . . It's not the mandate of the commission to go after anybody."

Zacklin referred *Newsday* to Vance and Owen. "He [Kalshoven] certainly met with Vance and Owen quite often," he said. "Could it have been Mr. Vance [who asked Kalshoven to limit his inquiry]? Could it have been Mr. Owen? It might well be that they have a position on that."

Vance through a spokesman last night denied that either he or Owen had tried to steer the commission away from investigating specific individuals. "They would not do any such thing as a matter of principle; and . . . they would not do anything to jeopardize the integrity of the peace process or their own credibility as impartial mediators," spokesman Fred Eckhard said.

Ambassador Herbert Okun, a deputy to Vance, told *Newsday* that Zacklin's intimation was "ridiculous" and "slanderous."

Eckhard said that Vance and Owen did influence Kalshoven once, by prodding to approve the only investigation associated with the commission. That is the planned exhumation of hundreds of corpses from a site outside Vukovar, reportedly Croat patients seized upon the Serbs' capture of a Vukovar hospital, stemming from the Serb-led attack on Croatia in 1991. To cover the $220,000 in costs, the U.S.–based Physicians for Human Rights had to solicit private donations, and again financier Soros signed the check.

While Vance and Owen vigorously reject suggestions that they influenced the war crimes probe, peace negotiations and the judicial process are on a collision course.

"It is a very tough call whether to point the finger or try to negotiate with people," commented Abram. "As a lawyer, of course, I would like to prosecute everybody who is guilty of these heinous things. As a diplomat or as a politician or as a statesman, I also would like to stop the slaughter, bring it to a halt. You have two things that are in real conflict here. . . . I don't know the proper mix."

None of this bodes well for the tribunal. The Security Council's February 19 resolution, which approved the tribunal in principle, did not provide for the appointment of a prosecutor or provide funds for a preliminary investigation, or even set a firm deadline for the final report on how the tribunal should be structured, which is to be prepared by Zacklin. Yet, according to commission members and Zacklin himself, in the absence of a prosecutor or funds, the tribunal, if it comes about, will have to rely at the beginning on Kalshoven's work.

Ron Howell and Dele Olojede at the United Nations in New York contributed to this story.

In May 1993 the Security Council approved a proposal by UN Secretary-General Boutros Boutros-Ghali for an international tribunal to examine war crimes in the former Yugoslavia. The guidelines stipulated that the tribunal should have the power to prosecute persons committing genocide and crimes against humanity. It stipulated that those subject to prosecution included "all persons who participate in the planning, preparation or execution of serious violations of international humanitarian law in the former Yugoslavia."

Three Who Planned Rape and Murder

Leader's Inner Circle Set Up Rape Camp in Muslim Town

Sarajevo, Bosnia-Herzegovina, April 19, 1993

Using flashlights and torches of lighted paper, the Serb military police stole through the darkened indoor sports center in search of female victims. Each night they selected 10 or more Muslim women. The men led them at gunpoint to a nearby house and raped them, witnesses and victims said. One 27-year-old woman told *Newsday* she was raped up to six times a night. Another woman was raped in the hall before the eyes of the others held there, witnesses said.

The site of these crimes, known as the Partizan sports hall, was in the center of Foca, a small, predominantly Muslim town in eastern Bosnia. At times, it was used as a transit facility for women and children about to be deported from the town. But for two months in 1992, between June and August, it functioned as a rape camp, holding 74 people, including about 50 women.

Partizan was one of dozens of Serb rape camps in Bosnia—some are said to be still in operation—and it was prominently located, next door to the police station. Muslim women victims said they complained about the routine raping to the police, but police said they had no power to intervene.

Power in Foca had been seized by three top associates of Bosnian Serb leader Radovan Karadzic. Velibor Ostojic, a minister in Karadzic's breakaway government, and two other close aides, Vojislav Maksimovic and Petar Cancar, organized the military assault on Foca in April 1992 and took charge of the town, even stationing their own guards in front of the police station.

Until now, reports on "ethnic cleansing" have focused on the men and women who implemented the policy—paramilitary groups led by self-promoting nationalists from neighboring Serbia aided by local Serb extremists. In Foca, the paramilitaries wore camouflage fatigues and called themselves the "Serbian Guard."

But a three-month *Newsday* investigation into ethnic cleansing in Foca suggests that those directing the process were members of Karadzic's inner circle. They called in paramilitary troops to conquer the town and gave the orders to "cleanse" Foca of all non-Serbs, a broad array of witnesses said. They set up concentration camps and rape camps, and on their orders, Serb forces destroyed the mosques and nearly every other sign of half a millenium of Muslim culture, according to a variety of government and Muslim sources.

Karadzic said in a telephone interview last week that he had no knowledge of systematic rape anywhere in Serb-conquered Bosnia. "We know of some 18 cases of rape altogether, but this was not organized but done by psychopaths," he told *Newsday*. Claims of mass rapes were "propaganda . . . designed" by "Muslim Mullahs," he added. (A special mission of the European Community estimated that 20,000 or more Bosnian Muslim women had been raped by Serb forces through the end of last year; numerous investigations by other governmental and nongovernmental organizations all have concluded that rape has been widespread.)

But he confirmed that Ostojic, Maksimovic and Cancar "influenced the establishment of civilian authorities" at the time of the military assault one year ago and took control of Foca. Karadzic has been described as a possible war criminal by former Secretary of State Lawrence Eagleburger.

In Sarajevo, the besieged capital of the devastated state of Bosnia, the Bosnian State Commission on War Crimes, headed by Croat Stjepan Klujic, is investigating all three men. Its allegations against Ostojic alone read like a page from the Nuremberg Nazi War Crimes Tribunal. It says Ostojic conceived and organized war crimes in the Foca region, helped plan and organize the arming of the Serbian Democratic Party members, prepared the attack and invited paramilitary forces from Serbia "to undertake the armed conquest of a large portion of the territory of Bosnia-Herzegovina and ethnic cleansing through annihilation, terror, persecution, detention, mistreatment and murder."

Ostojic refused to comment. A *Newsday* special correspondent in Belgrade submitted to Ostojic seven questions in writing about his role in the conquest of Foca in April 1992, asking him to describe the structure and authority of the crisis staff and to comment on the extensive eyewitness accounts of the rape camp in the middle of Foca.

The questions were submitted by fax at Ostojic's insistence, but after considering them for several days, he refused to reply. "I do not answer hypothetical questions," he said in a telephone interview. During a subsequent visit to Belgrade, he again refused to comment.

Bosnian Serb sources who spoke on condition of anonymity confirmed that Ostojic had been in Foca during the height of the terror and said he had traveled frequently to Pale, Karadzic's war headquarters on a mountain outside Sarajevo, for consultations.

Serb forces have denied foreign reporters and international organizations access to Foca since the conquest, and the *Newsday* investigation has relied on witnesses and victims now in Germany, Turkey, Bosnia-Herzegovina and the remaining Yugoslavia, as well as Bosnian officials in Sarajevo and abroad.

Seven victims at a refugee camp at Kirklareli, Turkey, and in southern Serbia retold the story of systematic rape in and around Foca and of the rape camp in the heart of the town. Written statements by 10 others were made available by the gynecologist who first examined the victims after their release last August. All statements were made on the condition that they not be identified. But current and former Bosnian government officials spoke on the record.

Foca, whose population of 40,000 was 52 percent Muslim and 45 percent Serb prior to the Serb conquest, was among the first towns Serb forces seized in Bosnia, and some observers believe that what happened there set a pattern for ethnic cleansing in the rest of Bosnia. Foca could be a case study in the role played by civilian politicians in the brutality against the non-Serb population.

According to a witness, Ostojic was spokesman for the conquering Serbs, while Maksimovic actually picked up the phone and called in the troops. For Ostojic, it was a familiar role. Prior to the Serb insurrection one year ago, he was minister of information in the coalition of Muslims, Serbs and Croats who ran the Bosnian government, and he held the same job in Karadzic's self-declared government of the "Serbian Republic" of Bosnia until January. Famed Nazi hunter Simon Wiesenthal, in an interview with *Newsday,* called him the "Goebbels" of the Bosnian Serbs. Currently Ostojic is a minister in Karadzic's government operating out of Pale. Karadzic and Ostojic were born in neighboring villages at the foot of Montenegro's Mount Durmitor but did not meet until 1990, Karadzic said. Both are 47.

Maksimovic was a professor of literature at the University of Sarajevo and the leader of Karadzic's Serbian Democratic Party in the Bosnian parliament. Karadzic has just named him head of the "University of the Serbian Republic," which he said will be established in Serb-controlled territory in Sarajevo. Cancar, an attorney, was formerly president of the chamber of municipalities, the second chamber of the Bosnia parliament. He is now a member of Karadzic's parliament.

According to Bosnian Muslim sources, Ostojic played a critical role in establishing a pattern of abuse of women.

Alija Delimustafic, who was Bosnia's interior minister at the time of the capture of Foca, said he had received direct evidence from wiretaps that proved Ostojic had ordered the raping of women in Foca. Delimustafic left the Bosnian government some months ago and is now working in Vienna as a private businessman.

Jusuf Pusina, Delimustafic's successor in Sarajevo, said he was unable to find any such evidence in his files and denied *Newsday* direct access to them. Although Delimustafic has been regarded in government circles with distrust since he quit his post, Kemal Kurspahic, editor of Sarajevo's independent daily newspaper, *Oslobodjenje,* said Delimustafic was a trustworthy source.

In a written statement to *Newsday,* Pusina did note, however, that Ostojic had been fired as a high school teacher for "his sexually deviant behavior toward young female pupils which on many occasions led to physical showdowns with individual parents." While employed in the personnel department at Sarajevo television, his next job, Ostojic "continued to satisfy his sick desire for girls by promising them 'certain work' if they fulfilled his desires," Pusina said. His last job was as proofreader at Sarajevo television, but he also had been Communist Party secretary.

Ostojic, who became a Karadzic protégé and was appointed by him to the Bosnian and Bosnian Serb governments, in fact used the incidents to advance his political career. In May 1991, the ministry said, Ostojic was beaten up on his doorstep by an angry husband, but he "and the extreme wing of the SDS [Karadzic's Democratic Party] built this up into a political thriller of a . . . Mujahedeen conspiracy that was the beginning of the night of the long knives against the Serbian princes," the ministry said.

Ostojic arrived in Foca around April 5 last year, three days before the attack, according to Enver Pilaff, 58, who at the time was head of the Muslim Democratic Action Party. At a public meeting, Ostojic demanded that Muslims give up all weapons of self-defense and concede that Foca was a Serbian territory.

"He gave the Muslims 15 minutes to think it over. But no one could agree because they didn't have the authority," said Pilaff, who subsequently fled to Sarajevo, where he was interviewed.

Ostojic then demanded that all Muslims leave Foca for a concentration camp at nearby Jabuka Mountain "or else the last Muslim seed will be destroyed in Foca," according to a public statement cited by the Bosnian Interior Ministry.

The next day, Ostojic, Maksimovic and Cancar met at their favorite restaurant, the Ribarski Dom. "I was outside when Maksimovic came out and told his people that if they would not take up arms and start shooting Muslims, he would call for reinforcements from Serbia," Pilaff said.

In the presence of his two associates, Maksimovic went to the telephone and "invited in" troops from nearby cities of Niksic in Montenegro, and Uzice in Serbia, Pilaff said. Pilaff said he heard the call through the open door.

"I said to the three of them: 'Aren't you ashamed for what you did?'" Pilaff said. As the first of 4,000 paramilitary troops arrived in trucks and buses, Pilaff and his family prepared to flee.

Molestation of Muslim women began almost immediately. On April 11, the third day after the attack on Foca, Pilaff said he heard from a close associate that a local Serb nationalist had raped a Muslim woman. Ostojic's forces also began rounding up Muslim civilians, taking them to the state correctional prison in Foca where the Bosnian government says more than 1,000 men were executed.

By mid-April, the trio set up their headquarters at a villa just outside Foca, next to the Velecevo state prison for women and overlooking the Cehotina River. There, guarded by several hundred paramilitary troops, they established a summary military court, witnesses said. *Newsday* has obtained a sworn statement by a former Yugoslav army officer of Muslim descent who said he was brought before them and other Serb leaders. On the advice of a senior Serb officer, they spared his life. According to other Bosnian state and Muslim party sources, Ostojic, Maksimovic and Cancar decided the fate of hundreds of Muslims in the area—whether they would be executed by the paramilitary forces or sent to the concentration camp at Foca prison. According to Pilaff and Muharem Omerdzic, an official of Riyaset, a Muslim benevolent association in Sarajevo, they then turned the women's prison at Velecevo into a women's concentration camp.

Both Pilaff and Omerdzic said their information came from refugees or the families of women still being held in Bosnia. Omerdzic said he believes those taken to Velecevo either were killed there or are still being held. He also estimated that thousands of Muslim women are still held in Serb camps inside Bosnia, where widespread rape continues. *Newsday* was unable to confirm their assertions.

Karadzic told *Newsday* he had not visited Foca since the conquest and was unaware that aides had set up their headquarters at Velecevo. He also said he had not known that Velecevo was the site of a women's prison. Karadzic said he had not heard that women had been held and systematically raped nightly over two months at Partizan hall. "We will investigate any allegations of rape, including this one," he said.

❖

A Daily Ritual of Sex Abuse

Kirklareli, Turkey, April 19, 1993

First, the Serb soldiers arrested Beba's husband and took him to a concentration camp in the southeast Bosnian town of Foca. Two months later, she said, armed Serb men returned to her village to rape the unprotected Muslim women left behind. Beba was raped. She fled to Foca, and there, from an apartment belonging to a Muslim family, she observed the daily ritual of sexual abuse at the Partizan sports center.

"I saw the same men entering and leaving daily" with women in tow, the 24-year-old Muslim woman, who asked to be identified by a fictitious name, told *Newsday*. "I can say in Foca there were 50 men involved in rape. They slept during the day and raped at night."

Beba's observations of organized and systematic rape over two weeks were corroborated by six other rape victims who spoke to a *Newsday* reporter at this refugee camp in Kirklareli, north of Istanbul, and in a predominantly Muslim town in southern Serbia.

Their accounts suggest that Serb authorities not only approved the systematic rape of Muslim women in Foca but made a public display of rape at Partizan hall. One woman at Partizan said she was raped more than 100 times in two months. A gynecologist who examined her shortly after her release told *Newsday* her account was entirely credible.

"The first rapes began a week or two after the Serb takeover in early April" last year, said Alija Delimustafic, who at the time was Bosnian interior minister. "They compiled lists. They arrested the men. They ordered women to stay in their home villages. They warned them they would kill their fathers or husbands if they moved away."

After an interval varying from a few weeks to two months, armed men in uniforms, either police reserves, militiamen or other paramilitary forces, combed the villages, conducting house-to-house "interrogations." According to several victims interviewed by *Newsday,* the "interrogations" began with questions about hidden weapons but were quickly transformed into rape at gunpoint.

Beba's husband was seized in May, and his fate is unknown. In mid-July, on the excuse that they were searching for weapons, the men, armed and in uniform, forced their way into the home of a 17-year-old girl and ordered her to accompany them to Beba's house. As Beba watched, she said, they raped the teenager.

Beba's turn came a few days later, and though she was caring for her newborn, she was taken along with the teenage girl to a house outside Foca and raped after a mock interrogation.

Beba escaped the ordeal by fleeing to Foca on her own and spent two weeks close to Partizan. Those brought to the former sports center by police were raped repeatedly for weeks on end. Far from intervening to halt the crime, victims said, local police sometimes referred some Muslim women to Partizan to await safe passage out of the region.

One 41-year-old woman said she had complained to police after a group rape in which uniformed men molested her and a close relative, aged 19. The police said there was no need to see a doctor "but that we should go to Partizan and wait for a convoy," said the woman, who asked to be identified by her initial "B." But after watching guards abduct four women from Partizan, B. and her relative fled and hid in the attic of relatives for a month.

M.C., a 28-year-old shopkeeper in Foca who asked to be identified only by her initials, had no escape. She told *Newsday* that Serbs attacked her village of Trosanj on June

3, and about 50 people, mostly women, were taken in trucks and private vehicles to a workers' barracks called Buk Bijela. "The raping began immediately. Twice that day," she said.

Then they were ordered for 10 days to a high school, where she was raped by three men, and finally to Partizan. Of the 74 people at Partizan, 50 were women and the rest children and some older people. About 30 younger women were the main targets. "Only the women over 50 were safe," M.C. said. "They always took the 10 youngest" from the sports hall, she said in an interview at a refugee center in Turkey. The woman said she was raped about 150 times during the two months of her ordeal.

After picking the women for the night, guards took them to a nearby apartment or house, victims said. On one occasion shortly before the main group was allowed to leave, a woman, 40, was raped in the middle of the hall. "The guard beat her. She cried," said a woman, 44, who asked to be identified only by her initials, R.C.

On August 12, guards ordered M.C. to an outdoor stadium where, she said, uniformed soldiers gang-raped her and other women. "I counted 29 of them. Then I lost consciousness," said the mother of two young children. When she came to, she heard the commander telling the troops: "Enough is enough." There was a quarrel, gunfire, and then the officer, who had taken part in the assault, drove her back to the Partizan sports hall.

The rapes within Partizan represent only a tiny fraction of the assaults against the Muslim women of Foca. There seemed to be a special regime for the prettiest and the smartest of the women, who were singled out for the most frequent raping, several witnesses said. They said those women have not been seen since.

"Four young girls from Partizan were taken away, never to return," said R.C. Three were teenagers—14, 16 and 17 years old. "When they take you away, they may kill you. So if you are raped, you feel lucky. At least you're alive," she said. R.C. acknowledged she had been raped, but would not say how many times.

The women kept in Partizan hall finally boarded buses organized by Serb authorities on August 13 and were taken to Montenegro, the first stop in what looks to be a permanent deportation. M.C. is relieved to be far from home. Of the hundreds of women who emerged alive after the ordeal of last summer, at least 40 had become pregnant and had abortions, and some had carried to term, according to a Muslim doctor in southern Serbia. "Everybody said that if we didn't move out of Foca, every second woman would be pregnant," added M.C.

❖

Serbs Bankroll Speeches
by Ex-UN Commander

United Nations, June 22, 1993

The former United Nations commander in Bosnia has taken part in a speaking tour funded by a Serbian-American advocacy group that seeks to dispel the internationally accepted view that Serb fighters were principally responsible for the mass killings, rape and "ethnic cleansing" that have destroyed the former Yugoslav republic.

In an interview with *Newsday*, retired Canadian Maj. Gen. Lewis MacKenzie said he has done nothing unethical or improper in connection with last month's tour. MacKenzie acknowledged in a telephone conversation from Ottawa that his tour was funded by the group, SerbNet, but said he didn't know how much he was paid. MacKenzie said that he customarily receives up to $10,000 an appearance and that he wouldn't be surprised if SerbNet paid that rate through his agent.

SerbNet later confirmed that it had paid him $15,000 plus expenses to give more than a dozen speeches and interviews in Washington two days last month.

In his public appearances, including congressional testimony last month, MacKenzie never disclosed SerbNet's financial support.

Accepting money from an advocacy group violates no laws or official policies of the United Nations, but a top UN official, who asked to remain anonymous, said, "We quite frankly are displeased with his lack of judgment."

MacKenzie, who served as the top UN peacekeeper in Bosnia from March to August 1992, argues that all the parties in the Balkans war are to blame for atrocities. "Dealing with Bosnia is a little bit like dealing with three serial killers—one has killed 15, one has killed 10, one has killed five," MacKenzie said in testimony before the House Armed Services Committee last month. "Do we help the one that's only killed five?"

That view puts MacKenzie at odds with reports by the UN, the United States and international human rights groups that have found the Serbs primarily responsible for the ethnic cleansing and mass killings. The State Department's own reports list 285 instances of war crimes, of which only 18 involved actions by Muslim forces. Serbian nationalist groups support MacKenzie's position, which tends to minimize the role of Serbian fighters.

SerbNet, short for the Serbian American National Information Network, was set up in Chicago "to articulate the Serb position" after adverse international publicity over alleged Serb atrocities against the Bosnian Muslims, said treasurer Milan Visnick. "Serbs have suffered mightily at the hands of the world media in the last year," he said. Its board consists largely of representatives of leading Serb nationalist organizations.

"We were very pleased that there was someone to speak more favorably of the Serbs," said Visnick of Mackenzie. In the latest issue of its monthly "Media Watch," the group portrayed the MacKenzie tour as the high point of the organization's most successful month yet in bringing the Serbian-American perspective before the wider public.

During his trip, MacKenzie, 53, gave more than a dozen speeches and interviews questioning the value of American military intervention to rescue Bosnia's Muslims. SerbNet said Mackenzie had appeared on the nationally broadcast Larry King television and radio talk shows, met the editorial board of *US News and World Report* and spoke with 10 reporters from the Associated Press Washington Bureau. He also gave interviews to the *Washington Times, National*

Journal, Time magazine, Gannett and ABC radio. He also met several leading *Washington Post* columnists and appeared on CNN.

During many appearances, Mackenzie made his oft-stated assertion that the vast majority of ceasefire violations that he observed in Bosnia were committed by the predominantly Muslim government forces. Other UN officers who served with him say that the assertion distorts the facts, because Serb gunners often took advantage of a ceasefire and staged moves that were deliberately provocative.

"My position is always one of objectivity because I don't blame only the Serbs," he told *Newsday*. "I'll continue to say things exactly the way I see them."

A spokesman for Secretary-General Boutros Boutros-Ghali said the UN had no problems with MacKenzie's actions. "The man is back in the service of his country and has nothing further to do with the UN," said Ahmad Fawzi, the spokesman. "If anything, the secretary-general would wish him good luck."

But others disagreed. "To be going on the road for Serbian organizations whose only purpose is propaganda—that, to me, crosses the line and is egregiously unethical," said George Kenney, a State Department official who resigned last year to protest U.S. government inaction in the face of Serb atrocities in the war. Kenney said while he was working at the State Department, officials there frequently were unable to find any factual basis for Mackenzie's statements alleging that government forces were firing at their own civilians.

Told of MacKenzie's dealings with SerbNet, Muhamed Sacirbey, the Bosnian government's envoy to the UN, said it proved that the former UN commander was partisan, even when he wore the UN blue beret. "General MacKenzie already exhibited his bias from the beginning," said Sacirbey. "It leaves the question of whether he was bought and paid for from the beginning."

There have been other public-relations campaigns in the war in Bosnia. The Bosnian government employed Ruder-Finn, a Washington public relations firm, in 1992, but a spokesman for the agency said the account is currently inactive. UN sanctions bar the Serbian-dominated rump Yugoslavia from hiring a public-relations firm, but the ban does not apply to Serbian-American groups. According to its own publications, SerbNet currently employs two leading public relations firms—McDermott/O'Neill & Associates, a liberal Democratic firm headed by Thomas P. O'Neill III, the son of the former House Speaker, and David A. Keene & Associates of Arlington, Virginia. Keene is chairman of the American Conservative Union. Both assisted in setting up MacKenzie's May media and speaking tour, according to officials of both firms.

Getting MacKenzie to make a tour in which he argued against U.S. military intervention in Bosnia was a propaganda coup for supporters of Bosnian Serbs. He was an authoritative and believable figure as the top UN commander in the former Yugoslav republic. A blunt and colorful soldier, MacKenzie has served, by his own count, in nine UN peacekeeping missions around the world, including assignments in the Middle East, Africa and Central America. As commander of the United Nations Protection Force, he was credited with keeping the Sarajevo airport open for relief flights at a time when the Serb siege of the city threatened thousands of people with starvation.

MacKenzie's popularity grew in Canada, and some newspapers compared him with Dwight Eisenhower—a general with a political future. One newspaper poll showed him tied in popularity with the Toronto Blue Jays, the first non-U.S. baseball team to win the World Series.

MacKenzie also came in for some criticism while he still served in the Canadian military. Gen. John de Chastelain, the head of the military, last autumn issued a reminder to MacKenzie, who had given a television interview, that official guidelines required him to seek permission before giving interviews or making speeches.

In late April, a month after MacKenzie retired, a member of Parliament from Calgary, Alex Kindy, raised a question in the Canadian House of Commons about the general's public appearances. "Who is paying for Mr. MacKenzie's trips? Is he a lobbyist? Is he a lobbyist for the Serbian side? These are questions which I think are very legitimate," Kindy said.

MacKenzie has long insisted that while Bosnian Serbs may have killed or raped or pillaged more than others, the image of Bosnian Muslims as victims is a false one. He pressed this view during an appearance before the U.S. House committee; in meetings with influential congressmen, including Sen. John Kerry (D-Mass.), a member of the Foreign Relations Committee; in a speech at the conservative Heritage Foundation; and in the newspaper interviews and television appearances. MacKenzie is also the featured celebrity in a half-hour film produced by SerbNet titled "Truth Is the Victim in Bosnia."

In his testimony before the House committee, MacKenzie argued for the creation of a small Muslim state in central Bosnia, while Croats and Serbs get their respective wishes for Greater Serbia and Greater Croatia. (European countries have signaled they will accept an ethnic partition of Bosnia that would consign Muslims to a landlocked territory around the capital of Sarajevo. President Bill Clinton indicated last week that, if the parties agree, he would have no objection.) MacKenzie also said Western military intervention would fail.

"If the aim is not to right all of the wrongs of the past, which is clearly impossible, but to stop the killing and to create the conditions for a lasting peace in Bosnia-Herzegovina, we had better admit it's too late to put Bosnia back together again," he concluded.

MacKenzie said an April trip he took to Belgrade was at the invitation of Bosnian Serb leader Radovan Karadzic. He said the visit with Karadzic—an accused war criminal, according to the State Department—was made only to secure passage for Canadian troops being prevented by Serbian militiamen from entering Srebrenica to monitor the Security Council's safe area plan.

MacKenzie said the flak he has taken was to be expected in such a conflict. Any UN commander, he said, would be similarly accused by all sides.

"I have spoken to over 450 groups, from India to the U.S., from Boy Scouts to all 14 NATO countries, all at their request," he said. "I have spoken to Muslim and Croat organizations in places like Chicago and Detroit. I speak in objective terms and condemn all sides."

"It's a damnable lie to say he was in our pocket," Nicholas Trkla, national coordinator for SerbNet, said. "We just made sure he had the opportunity to make his views known." Trkla also insisted that SerbNet was not an advocacy group for Bosnian Serbs, something he said was prohibited by law because SerbNet is registered as a not-for-profit organization.

"To infer that we are a front organization for the Yugoslav government is absolutely false," Trkla said. "We just want the truth."

An expanded version of a story co-authored
with staff correspondent Dele Olojede.

Epilogue

Ten days before Germany invaded Poland in 1939, Adolf Hitler summoned his top military commanders to his Obersalzberg eyrie to divulge his intentions once they completed the military conquest. His plan called for Nazi-style "ethnic cleansing."

"Poland will be depopulated and settled with Germans," Hitler said in the secret speech. Just as Genghis Khan had "sent millions of women and children into death knowingly and with a light heart," Hitler said he had commanded the SS Death's Head formations to kill without mercy or pity "many women and children of Polish origin and language." Only thus "can we gain the living space that we need. Who after all is today speaking about the destruction of the Armenians?"

The speech so shocked the audience that one admiral present smuggled highlights to the British embassy in Berlin in a vain attempt to head off the butchery.

Historical precedent gave Hitler reason to think he would be able to get away with genocide in Poland, and the spineless behavior of Western politicians bolstered his confidence. "I experienced those poor worms Daladier and Chamberlain in Munich," he told his commanders, referring to the British and French prime ministers, Neville Chamberlain and Edouard Daladier. "They will be too cowardly to attack. They won't go beyond a blockade." [1]

The Allies did fight back in self-defense, and after defeating Germany, they set the historic precedent of organizing

[1] *Documents on British Foreign Policy 1919–1939*, 3rd Series, VII. London:1954, pp. 257–260. The original text as sent to the Foreign Office August 25, 1939.

the International War Crimes Tribunal at Nuremberg. Yet Hitler's assumption about genocide proved right.

Half a century later, Serbia's war in Bosnia demonstrates that a regional power with a ruthless leader, military superiority and an extreme nationalist ideology can carry out "ethnic cleansing" on European soil if it does not directly challenge the interests of a major power. This time, the intentions were divulged not in a leaked secret speech but in an accumulation of news reports and documentation by Western governments and international relief agencies. Even while the conflict raged, the UN Security Council agreed to a war crimes tribunal to try those suspected of genocide and crimes against humanity. But like spectators of a television miniseries, the United States and Europe continued to watch passively as the crimes were being committed.

Some view the passivity as a loss of compass by a generation of weak leaders at the dawn of the new era. In the aftermath of the Cold War, the collapse of Communism in Europe, and the dismantling of the Soviet Empire, events moved so fast that the United States, as sole remaining superpower, and its allies had not perfected a framework to replace the bipolar world or established a policy-making mechanism to go with it. There is ample evidence, however, to trace Western indifference to the U.S. decision to look away when the crisis began. Whatever the cause, the West faces a fiasco in the Balkans, in large part of its own making. Having recognized a country with a civil order, the world community refused to let it defend its sovereignty or its people and abandoned it to the aggressor.

However unpredictable the Balkans may be, experts agree that the crisis cannot be contained in Bosnia-Herzegovina. The virus of aggressive nationalism is spreading unchecked, and long-suppressed forces have been unleashed. Conflict can explode at any time, whether in Kosovo, in Macedonia or Croatia, and lead to a European war. The choice before the West is whether to let aggression against Croatia and Bosnia-Herzegovina stand, ushering in a return to the darkest period of modern history, or to restore some sort of order similar to the relative calm of the Cold War's waning years. If the West is to regain influence over events in southeastern Europe and avoid a reversion to the law of the jungle in which might makes right, its leaders will have to draw lessons from their mistakes and reexamine their principles. Some lessons should have been self-evident.

America's involvement or non-involvement in European affairs has proven to be a key factor in peace and war. The two major wars of the century began in Europe while the United States was in isolation, and U.S. military intervention proved the key to the outcome of both. The West's clear victory in the third and longest conflict, the 45-year Cold War against the Soviet bloc, would have been unimaginable without U.S. leadership.

Twin blunders by the Bush administration in 1991 probably doomed the West's response from the time the Balkan crisis erupted. U.S. political leaders ignored the signs that the breakup of Yugoslavia was unavoidable, and instead of devising a strategy to deal with reality, withdrew to the sidelines and foreswore the use of force. The argument was made that the Balkans held little strategic importance for the United States in comparison to Kuwait because there was no oil in Bosnia-Herzegovina; yet it is folly to think that stability in Central Europe is not in the United States's strategic interest, recalling the origins of two World Wars. For their part, U.S. military leaders disregarded the evidence of outright aggression and lazily accepted the propaganda line put out by the Serb-led Yugoslav army that any intervention would land the West in another Vietnam. They were reinforced in their preferred course by the private and public advice proffered by Lewis MacKenzie, the retired UN commander, who became the self-appointed leading Western military "expert" opposing intervention. Despite his former title, MacKenzie was not neutral. After retiring from the Canadian army with the rank of major-general, he went on the payroll of Serbian-American nationalist supporters of the Serb conquest.

Having given up a political and/or military role, the United States could not regain its leadership, and European diplomacy became a throwback to the League of Nations. The only tools available to the League, economic sanctions and the non-recognition of conquest, proved no match for dictators in the 1930s. The League failed to stop the series of land-grabs that led up to the Second World War—Japan's seizure of Manchuria in 1931, Italy's annexation of Ethiopia in 1936, or Germany's takeover of the Rhineland that same year—and the weakness of the world body may indirectly have encouraged the aggression. After Britain and France agreed to Hitler's carve-up of Czechoslovakia in 1938, the League collapsed.

The UN-sponsored negotiations on Bosnia-Herzegovina, operating out of the League's Palais des Nations in Geneva, relied on the same tools and ended up with a similar result.

There was more déjà vu in the West's attitude to refugees. In July 1938, Adolf Eichmann, in charge of the Nazi "Central Office for Jewish Emigration" in Vienna, sent an offer to an international conference on refugees at Evian-les-Bains, France, to save the lives of the 180,000 Jews of Vienna for $400 per head, or, if there were no takers, $200 a head. The United States refused to raise its immigration quota, and other countries followed its example, thus setting the stage for the Nazi "Final Solution" for the Jews of Central Europe.[2]

In Bosnia, the United States and Europe opened their doors a crack to admit concentration camp survivors, but largely let the burden of more than 200,000 refugees fall on Croatia. When Croatia closed its borders, the West stayed silent. That was a signal to Serb nationalists to carry on with their mad design.

If there is one lesson that the post–World War II generation

---

[2] Recounted in *Stella*, by Peter Wyden. New York: Simon & Schuster, 1992, pp. 54–65.

now taking control of Western governments learned from the Nazi Holocaust against European Jewry, it is that genocide must never again be permitted to occur in Europe. In the absence of U.S. leadership, however, there appears to be no way to stop it.

Hitler could boast in 1939 that no one remembered the destruction of the Armenians thanks in part to U.S. policy shifts in the early 1920s. Under Allied pressure, but especially that of the U.S. ambassador to Istanbul, Henry Morgenthau, Turkey's pro-Western government indicted hundreds of nationalists at the end of World War I for organizing and carrying out genocide against an estimated one million Armenians. But after a change of administrations in Washington and with the rise of "Young Turk" nationalist Kemal Ataturk, the United States shifted priorities, dropping its humanitarian concerns in favor of purely economic interests as it sought a share in the oil fields of the Ottoman Empire. As U.S. commercial interests competed for advantage against Britain and France, U.S. diplomats argued against prosecuting crimes against humanity on the technical ground that no such crime existed under international law. The trials halted.

A strong U.S. commitment was a critical factor in establishing the Nuremberg proceedings after World War II, with Morgenthau, then Franklin Roosevelt's Secretary of the Treasury, pressing hardest. But American business interests eager to recoup their investments played an influential role in averting trials of leading German industrialists, despite compelling evidence they had profited from the use of slave labor from concentration camps.[3]

After the genocide in Kampuchea, no country came forth to demand war crimes proceedings against the Khmer Rouge,

[3] Christopher Simpson, *The Splendid Blond Beast, Money, Law and Genocide in the Twentieth Century*, New York: Grove Press, 1993, pp. 27–37; and Cherif Bassiouni, "The Time Has Come for an International Criminal Court," *Indiana International & Comparative Law Review*, Vol. 1 No. 1, Spring 1991, pp. 2–3.

and for a time, after Vietnam invaded Kampuchea, the United States even sent financial support to the Khmer Rouge.

A return of U.S. leadership in Europe implies a recognition of the reality that the only way to deal with force is with counterforce. The West had ample opportunities to let the Bosnians rescue their state and people merely by supplying them with arms. In the view of many independent observers on the ground, the situation did not require a Western ground intervention, but Bosnia did need weapons to offset the immense Serb advantage and a guarantee of support against cross-border intervention by Serbia. Western countries postponed the decision, however, while negotiations continued. When Bosnian Serbs rejected the result of the mediation, the United Nations walked away from its own proposal. Britain and France refused to reconsider the arms ban. Thus the West abandoned Bosnia and consigned victory to the "ethnic cleansers."

In deciding where and how to reassert leadership, the United States can draw on the tried and tested principles developed by the Conference on Security and Cooperation in Europe, sometimes called the Helsinki principles. The CSCE forum is one of the unsung diplomatic achievements of the Cold War era; the principles evolved over 15 years facilitated the peaceful transition in the former Soviet empire from Communist dictatorship to fledgling democracy. CSCE members agreed unanimously to oppose the change of borders by force, to ensure minority rights, to observe Western-style human and civil rights and to have a free exchange of goods, services, and information. Formally, the CSCE, consisting of all Europe plus the United States and Canada, agreed in July 1992 to transform itself into the primary authority in Europe on security threats, with power to authorize military responses by NATO or other European security bodies. Little came of the plan, which had the misfortune to be announced during the American presidential election campaign.

It will be the job of statesmen to rebuild the international system after the self-inflicted damage of the early 1990s. It will be up to the news media to watchdog the statesmen and discomfort the governments. The Balkan crisis is a reminder of the limits of the craft of journalism. In 1939, Admiral Wilhelm Canaris, the head of German counterintelligence, used intermediaries to send the warning to Britain of Hitler's secret plans in Poland, but the man who delivered the message to the mission was Louis Lochner, the bureau chief of the Associated Press in Berlin. Without identifying his source, Lochner told Ambassador Neville Henderson that it came from someone who "hoped for the curbing of a maniac." But British diplomats were immersed in frantic round-the-clock efforts to find a negotiated solution to German-Polish tensions; and the Embassy forwarded the text to the Foreign Office with a dismissive cover note, stating that the remarks were "interesting" but for "private consumption" and "such disposal as is fitting." Lochner published it in 1942. Then as now, the messenger can only carry the message.

In the Balkan crisis, European and American leaders wasted time and distracted public attention as they searched for a negotiated solution where none was available. To dampen public concerns, they denied the visible facts as amply reported in the news media. Imputing moral equivalency to aggressor and victim, they revised history to cover up their indecision. But that sort of response has always proved to be shortsighted. At best it postpones the day of reckoning, albeit at a cost of perhaps tens of thousands of lives. Western leaders need only recall the dictum of George Santayana that "those who disregard the past are bound to repeat it." Statesmen will have to decide if "ethnic cleansing" will be Europe's future as well as past. Sooner or later, they will have to face the reality of southeastern Europe, a situation they have allowed to run out of control.